Diary of a Novel

Also by Eugenia Price

FICTION

St. Simons Trilogy

Lighthouse
New Moon Rising
The Beloved Invader

Florida Trilogy

Don Juan McQueen
Maria
Margaret's Story

Savannah Quartet

Savannah
To See Your Face Again
Before the Darkness Falls
Stranger in Savannah

Georgia Trilogy

Bright Captivity

NONFICTION

Discoveries
The Burden Is Light
Early Will I Seek Thee
Share My Pleasant Stones
Woman to Woman
What Is God Like?
Beloved World
A Woman's Choice
God Speaks to Women Today
The Wider Place
Make Love Your Aim
Just as I Am

Learning to Live from the Gospels
The Unique World of Women
Learning to Live from the Acts
St. Simons Memoir
Leave Yourself Alone
Diary of a Novel
No Pat Answers
Getting Through the Night
What Really Matters
Another Day
At Home on St. Simons

Diary of a Novel

by **EUGENIA PRICE**

TURNER
PUBLISHING COMPANY

Turner Publishing Company

Nashville, Tennessee

www.turnerpublishing.com

Diary of a Novel

Cover design: Bruce Gore

Library of Congress Cataloging-in-Publication Data Upon Request

9781684427512   *Paperback*
9781684427529   *Hardback*
9781684427536   *eBook*

Printed in the United States of America

17 18 19 20 10 9 8 7 6 5 4 3 2 1

For the descendants of Margaret Seton Fleming,
especially Dorothy Fleming Austin,
the late Margaret Seton Fleming Biddle,
and Hester Fleming Williams

Part One

September 13, 1978
St. Simons Island, Georgia

The day toward which I've worked for more than a year will be here when the sun comes up over the back marsh tomorrow morning: *I leave for St. Augustine, Florida, to begin research for a new novel.* Aside from the fact that in another way I love the ancient little city as much as I love St. Simons Island, I will once more be able to breathe what has come to be my "native air"— historic novels.

Of course, it is gratifying that enough readers like them for me to make my living by writing. Although I am usually deplorably behind with correspondence, contact with those readers is my writer's lifeline. But today I am letting the unanswered letters go for a time. I am thinking only about me and my novel—and feeling no guilt.

At this beginning stage, I am not even allowing myself to remember that those dark days will come when the mountains of manila folders filled with documents and maps and genealogies will appear to be falling on me. Smothering me. I am also refusing to remember that in spite of having done it five times, the equally dark days will come when I'm dead certain that I'm just not up to handling such a huge canvas as a long novel. Especially one based on the actual lives of people who lived against the background of times far removed from now. Years which must become as familiar to me as this year of 1978 and next year, 1979, and part of 1980—depending upon how swiftly or how slowly the manuscript grows. None of that matters today. Today I am only lyrical.

I have settled on a story—the life of Margaret Seton Fleming, who lived her adult life in the last century, in a great white country house on the St. Johns River between Green Cove Springs and Orange Park in Florida—a remarkable life which spanned the Seminole wars and the Civil War. As with the main characters in my other novels, I am already convinced that I can live with Margaret day in and day out for whatever time is required to put her very human life on paper. Much of the research has already been done for me by two key persons—Dena Snodgrass, one of Florida's most respected historians, and Margaret's great-granddaughter, Hester Williams—and still knowing so little about the facts myself, I am excited to be escaping into the world of Hibernia on the St. Johns, Margaret's home. Writing a long novel is the hardest work I ever do, but I'm restless, jittery, never quite at home anywhere unless I'm at work on one. And to think I didn't discover this about myself until I was in middle life. Well, I know it now.

Writing the *St. Simons Memoir* this past year was fun and meaningful. Writing *Leave Yourself Alone* during the late summer and autumn did so much for me that if it doesn't light up for a single reader, the months spent on it will still have been valid. But now? Oh, now. I'm *home*. Another novel. Glory be.

September 14

The mood of exhilaration is contagious. Not only is my recently silent, totally eccentric mockingbird singing today as I pack to leave but my longtime friend Dot Madden is making a special trip into the beauty shop just to cut my almost forgotten hair. "I wouldn't think of holding you up if you're ready to begin work on another novel," she laughed. She's right. No one had better try. I doubt that anyone will who knows me at all. Knowing me at all means the sure knowledge that I'm a far more amenable person at this happy stage.

September 15
St. Augustine— 4 P.M.

I'm here. I'm here in my favorite little room at the Marion Motor Lodge on the Bay front. Paradox: Couldn't wait to get here but made the trip last as long as possible. I spurn interstates when I can, and so I took A-1A through Fernandina for a fish at The Surf, then the St. Johns River ferry and south past some of Don Juan McQueen's many properties, to South Ponte Vedra, where Maria Evans's land lay green and lush across the North River. (To me, so much of the north Florida land still "belongs" to Maria and Don Juan, whose stories I told in the first two novels in the Florida trilogy.)

Awareness increased as I drove along. . .joy and sadness. Joy springs from this new beginning. But, I will never begin another novel without the sadness. The missing. My beloved friend and historian par excellence, Walter C. Hartridge—and my late editor, Tay Hohoff, both so irrevocably a part of anything I'll ever write. Both are gone now and daily I'm glad that I know about the Great Going On. That knowledge is the cause for this deep certainty, as I write, that both Tay and Walter know I'm here in this familiar little room—ready to begin again.

Meaning deepened still more as I drove along toward St. Augustine and deepens this minute because of Walter Hartridge's great gift to me beyond his historian's expertise and enthusiasm for what I try to do in these novels. The gift? Dena. Dena Snodgrass—and she will arrive day after tomorrow from Jacksonville. Dena, my friend. One of Florida's truly prominent authorities on the state's history—economist, pedagogue, charming lady, mercurial mind, beautiful face and being, researcher supreme— and delightful kook. All of these? Yes. More. And the "more" is of the essence for me: She already knows, as though born knowing, as much about the problems of a novelist handling history as any-

15

one could know who isn't one.

Best of all, she is no age and all ages.

Walter's giving went on through Dena, who, in turn, has given me lovable Hester Williams, Margaret Seton Fleming's great-granddaughter. Hester is the other key person, who, with Dena, has already labored long over historical chronologies and who has made for me a family genealogical chart which, I know right now, will become my "bible" as I work through each day.

And here I sit in total, happy confusion with all this material, collected by Dena and Hester over the past six weeks, spread crazily across my motel room—bed, chairs, desk, floor. I'm certain that I will never absorb it all, but I'm not minding a bit because there will come that time when the creative process takes over and the novel begins. Right now, I'm reveling in Fatio and Fleming and Sibbald and Seton family histories, maps (though maps always cause me despair) and pages and pages of photocopied letters which will give me a picture of plantation life before, during and after the Civil War.

Mostly, right now, I am just here in blissful disarray. This afternoon I shall attempt to organize all the material—file it in folders—at my favorite spot in St. Augustine, the Historical Society Library on Charlotte Street (just around the corner from "Maria's house," known to tourists as The Oldest House.) Eugenia Arana, Mary Ellen Fabal and Jackie Bearden will be at the library to greet me with open arms and I them. Lifting the heavy iron latch on that handsome old gate at the Society library symbolizes joy to me. Irrational? Of course. But I can't lift it unless I'm *here* in St. Augustine, and being here means I'm away from desk work and the telephone–away free to adventure through a new story and to learn about the characters who will make it happen. (Never mind that I'm not the world's greatest writer. The world's greatest couldn't enjoy it more.)

September 16
Evening

There are nine thick manila folders somewhat sorted now.

The library's worktables are wonderfully long and roomy. I could spread out. Sorting the materials at this stage was, as always, confusion, confusion. In the late afternoon one thick bundle containing the romantic letters of a married couple whose lives rather paralleled the Flemings' lives, just disappeared. I knew I had it. I'd read some of the letters. *It wasn't there.* Dumbfounded, laughing, repeating still again the researcher's plaint of how material vanishes right under one's eyes, Jackie, Mary Ellen and I searched for over half an hour. At last, because it was closing time, I packed up and walked back to the motel, and there was the bundle of letters, where I suppose letters from a loving couple belong—on the bed!

Just sitting here in my room now in happy distraction, thinking not very coherent thoughts: Pushing down with enormous deliberateness the obvious fact that I am far from at home in my material at this early stage. Wondering almost idly about how to handle this and that, knowing full well that it is too early to wonder; The St. Johns River, by the way, runs *north* and so, to Floridians of the area, to go south on it is to go "upriver" and to go north toward Jacksonville is to go "downriver." A way must come to handle this so as not to confuse my readers. The way hasn't come yet.

An interesting fact: Many persons to whom I speak about Margaret Seton Fleming's difficult life during the American Civil War are startled that Florida was a Con- federate state. To them, Florida, of course, has always "belonged" to Yankees. It is a place for Yankees to go in winter. And so it was in Margaret's time.

Another interesting fact which I've just remembered is that I almost decided *against* Margaret's story. Excited as I am now, as much as I already love Margaret Seton Fleming and her family, two years ago I turned the story down. Dena had sent me a copy of *Hibernia, The Unreturning Tide*, by an imaginative lady named Margaret Seton Fleming Biddle—my Margaret's granddaughter. At the time, since *Maria* and *Don Juan McQueen* were both laid there, I was determined to find a story for the third in the Florida trilogy which would be set early in the American Territorial

17

years right in St. Augustine proper. But after much digging and many ideas from friends, no bells rang. In a way that is extremely hard to explain, a novelist who writes about real people must sense deeply that those people can be lived with for two full years if necessary. There must also be a story strong enough to support an entire book. A few of the suggestions made to me during those months were excellent in part—but not right. At least, not right for me.

Then, before my *St. Simons Memoir* came out, I was interviewed by Ann Hyman, prizewinning journalist for the Florida *Times-Union*, who had not only visited Margaret Fleming's homesite and her little church at Hibernia on the St. Johns, but who used the kind of persuasion one writer accepts from another. She had written a Sunday feature on Margaret and the church. Once I read Ann's story, I was convinced that I should at least reconsider. I did and here I am, full of gratitude to Ann Hyman and her superb story sense—more flexible than my own.

I remember sharply the morning—sometime during the writing of *St. Simons Memoir*—when I found myself welcoming Margaret Seton Fleming into my own life. Deliberately, I laid the *Memoir* manuscript aside, took the little Hibernia book off the shelf and read again the section on Margaret and Lewis Fleming. The more I read, the more I marveled that I had been so sure this was not my story. The section in Mrs. Biddle's book is called Lewis Fleming. But, it was his wife's story—at least for me. Margaret, a small, slender, tawny-haired young woman of Scottish descent, whose dark brown eyes had been arresting enough so that they were remarked upon more than a hundred years later in a family memoir, now took me by the heart. Born into a well-to-do merchant family from Long Island, who, because of their British loyalties in the American Revolution, had fled to the safety of the British colony of Florida, Margaret's years (she was born in Fernandina, Florida, in 1813) *spanned exactly the time frame in which I wanted to work*. What difference did it make that all of the story was not laid in St. Augustine? I now know that my own pleasure in working at the St. Augustine Historical Society Library—the only such place which suited me in all ways—had been one of my reasons for wanting a story laid only in St. Augustine. But because the Fleming family (Margaret married Lewis Fleming) was closely related to the Fatio family, I would be able to do at least some research in the relaxed, comfortable atmosphere of the library on Charlotte Street. And what would stop me from making St. Augustine my headquarters when a trip to north Florida was indicated? After all, the ancient city is only a half-hour's drive from the site of Hibernia. Now, in my present state of anticipation, I quake that I allowed already established work habits, which had been so satisfactory during the research and writing of the first two novels in the Florida trilogy, to close my mind to Margaret's richly lived story. I had not read more than five pages in *Hibernia, The Unreturning Tide* this time when I knew I not only could live with Margaret Seton Fleming for a long, long time—but that I was hearing those now familiar bells!

Born to comfort, her highly romantic, colorful adult life was a novelist's dream of both joy and sorrow. I already knew well from readers' letters that in these times of unsteady marriages a certain type of reader longs for a novel in which genuine romance—especially one which really happened—could be found. That Margaret Seton and Lewis Fleming loved as few love, no one could doubt. At least, I didn't. And this was true, in spite of the fact that Mrs. Biddle had rather skimmed over their romance. Good, I thought. This gives me all the freedom needed to build a novel. What the little privately published Hibernia book did give me was some usable facts and a colorful feel for the locale, the mystique of Hibernia itself—the Fleming plantation under the giant oaks and magnolias beside the mighty St. Johns River. I have never intended it so, but in each of my five earlier novels a place—a locale, a house or both—has assumed enormous importance to the story, I suppose because places are important to me. During that morning's reading, I began to sense that Margaret's story could hold the same fascination for readers as my first novel. *The Beloved Invader*, laid in the part of St. Simons Island where I now live. Readers, after more than fifteen years since *Invader*'s publication, still stream to Christ Churchyard, copies of my book in hand, to find the graves of the people about whom I wrote in *Invader*. Margaret Seton Fleming had even built her own little chapel in the woods near her house! But, Margaret herself, as much as her story—the beauty of her Hibernia setting, the strength of her romance, a rare blend of laughter and tears—had already begun to live with me!

I sat for a long time that morning, learning the ways in which she was different from the main character in my novel *Maria*. Both were strong women who left their mark on their society as few women did in those days, and yet they were unlike. Margaret Seton Fleming was that almost unique mixture—a romantically loving wife, an excellent manager, a superb mother. Oh, I admit that the fact that when she married Lewis Fleming she became the stepmother of three children by his first wife, Augustina, and then went on to have seven more of her own almost stopped me again. But each child would be different—one from the other—if I could bring it off. In this era of small families, stories about large numbers of children seem strange. Still, I spend money and time and energy seeing to it that my historical and genealogical facts are accurate—why flinch at the fact that in those days people did have large families?

That Margaret was ambitious, as was Maria, attracted me to her. That tourists were already pouring into Florida from the North interested me. They were coming as early as 1830. That Margaret took full advantage of this and persuaded Lewis to build a thirty-roomed house in which she could not only make money for the family but share that colorful, loving, very human family life with carefully selected paying guests—sealed the story for me. This novel would have perhaps more of the flavor my readers have liked in the other five, but an even richer, fuller story line.

At that early stage, with one book to finish and another to write before I could begin, I felt so drawn to Margaret that I had to put down a small inner rebellion toward the work to be done first. Her joys were supreme—her losses devastating. Out of the skeletal events of her life would surely come a theme which could tie the novel together. I had no idea what that theme would be—

but it would come. And in the interim, I could think about Margaret, allow her to become more real to me—learn her reactions, her strengths, her faults—in those night moments alone when the light was out. I could think about her, ponder her, driving to and from the store, the post office. At least, we had come together. All I did not know, I could learn or imagine or let happen once I was free to get into the actual research.

Of course, Dena Snodgrass was my gold mine for con- tacts and research. I called her the instant my mind was made up, and she went right to work. There was certainly much to be done. The story spans two wars—the Second Seminole War and the Civil War. And with such a large family, someone had to go through the (to me) agonies of a genealogical chart. But first, we felt that Dena should contact her friend Hester Williams (Mrs. Herbert) of Jacksonville, Margaret's great-granddaughter. Mrs. Biddle, who wrote the lovely little family book about Hibernia, is elderly and no longer lives in the South, but I had learned from practical experience that unless I have the enthusiasm of the descendants of a character behind me, it is far better to forget the whole idea. Dear, genteel, and determined Hester Williams made all the necessary contacts and found full approval. Most importantly, she set to work at once with Dena on research for me. For weeks, while I finished another manuscript and cleared my desk, these two friends worked, and I mean *worked*.

This mountain of manila folders crammed with the background of my novel is the result of their labors. I have tried in many ways to show my gratitude. I fear that I have failed. And here in print for them to read, along with all those who aided them (Norma Lockwood, in particular), is my word that even beyond the marvelous research material, I value their continuing understanding and enthusiasm.

Dena and Hester and Norma Lockwood, all active in the historical work of the National Society of Colonial Dames of America in the State of Florida, already had much that we needed. After all, the Fleming family and the Fatio family were irrevocably tied together all the way from the British period in Florida through the second Spanish period and into the American takeover. And, of course, throughout the Civil War and after. We began to find that some of the work would be lightened because so much excellent research had already been done by Dena, Hester and Norma Lockwood—all Florida Dames—on the history of the St. Augustine house owned by the Dames and known now as the Ximenez-Fatio house. These ladies have labored for years tracing the evolution of this handsome old building and its owners. At the peak of the tourist trade in the years before the Civil War, Louisa Fatio had owned the house and operated it as a "home away from home" for Northern guests visiting in St. Augustine. Lewis Fleming's father, George, had married into the wealthy, genteel Fatio family, and for years, the Fleming plantation at Hibernia had as its neighbors the Fatios just across the St. Johns River at New Switzerland. As time went on, I was sure to find a way to tie St. Augustine into the story, undoubtedly through Louisa Fatio herself. What Dena didn't know about the background of these two families so integral to my story, Hester or Norma did. All three immediately became involved in my problems. In fact, today, when I walked into the Historical Society Library, there sat Norma doing research that would help me! The research for this novel could turn out to be the most fascinating and complex research I've tackled yet. Mainly, it will be complex because there were *so many children*. (Still, I even have permission from descendants to omit entire branches of the family in order to save both my readers' sanity and my own!)

I feel certain as I sit here in my motel room writing, that Louisa Fatio, once the owner of the big house just a narrow St. Augustine street away, will somehow become important to the story. I already like her. She never married and so saves me more children to cope with.

Perhaps most strongly, in Margaret's story, I was drawn by the drama, the deep, painful scars left on her life by the Civil War. The war which I had never thought much about—in Florida. Indeed, Florida was unique among the Confederate states. The Hibernia story gives me fresh American history to work on, and Margaret's faith, her courage in withstanding her heavy losses—both material and personal—intrigues me. Over and over, she bounced back from the tragedies which began to strike her before the war. Then there was an ultimate tragedy and she collapsed. At this early stage. I'm not at all sure how I'll handle her return to hope—but I will. She did return.

Another purely incidental and subjective reason for my pleasure at doing this particular story is that Margaret

Seton Fleming was also an antecedent of Susan and Walter Hartridge and the superb contemporary writer Madeleine L'Engle. I'm not sure how much space I'll have for the L'Engle relatives, but in the South, families still matter—whether mentioned by name or not. It is a special balm to my heart because I think it is balm for Susan Hartridge's heart too that we both know dear Walter is excited right now that I'll be writing about the Fatios and the Flemings.

Today at the library, Norma Lockwood located the first Fatio house on the Bay (right where Potter's Wax Museum stands today) and also the site of the town house of George Fleming, Margaret's father-in-law. It stood near my motel, on the present site of Captain Jack's Restaurant, where I've found a chef's salad to my liking.

September 17
Dena has just arrived—full of energy, excitement, knowledge and cheer. We will work! Oh, how we will work.

September 19
Now, it is late Tuesday afternoon and Dena has just pulled away in her neat little blue Pacer, headed back to her home in Jacksonville after having spent two whole days and most of two nights in concentrated study with me. We took time out only for meals—one at The Chart House, one at the Santa Maria across Avenida Menendez—the rest I've forgotten, because everything we did other than "talk Margaret" escapes me. As Dena kissed me good-bye, she said: " I feel as though I've been grilled for two days by a hotshot DA!" I may never see her exhausted again. I know I am now, but so absorbed by the story that I plan, as soon as

23

this entry is down on paper, to go through all the material—just once more. It is a source of plain old pride to me that Dena was impressed with how much I've already absorbed of the history of the Fatios and the Flemings. She did manage to gather up her copies of all the research, but mine are still spread on the floor, across two chairs and on the bed. Each day, for eleven hours, slowly, painstakingly, we began to fit together the pieces of the puzzle. Even so, she left with a sheaf of questions for still further research. I was up by six today, and Dena in my room for coffee by seven. Lest all this sound grim and harrowing, it isn't. I don't remember laughing so much or so often—especially when at the same instant both of us drew blanks on points which we knew perfectly well. Also, when we "lost" entire folders of material.

The highlight, though, was time spent inside the famous Fatio house on Aviles Street.

I had already definitely decided that it was more than plausible in spite of fifteen years difference in their ages (perhaps because of it—Margaret, the younger) that Louisa Fatio and Margaret Fleming would be confidantes. Dena and Hester agreed. Certainly, after Louisa purchased the large, handsome house on Aviles Street (then called Hospital Street), Margaret would have visited her often in St. Augustine. (Much to be done yet on exactly how Margaret made this trip from Hibernia on the St. Johns and across to St. Augustine.) At any rate, Louisa Fatio, a handsome, practical, loving woman, will be in the story. And so, for two hours, alone in "Louisa's house," we let our imaginations run wild, curbed only by what Dena already knew of the customs of the times. From 1855 until her death in 1875 Louisa ran the house as an inn for Northern tourists and it was one of the most desirable in the city. So Dena reenacted for me, as we sat together in what had been Louisa's upstairs parlor, the arrival of "three or four guests from the North." Louisa, before our visit to "her" house ended, was so real to me, I could already "hear" her voice!

Tonight, dinner with the kind and charming Kaczmarczyks, Stephanie and Horst, who own the motel where I stop. Now, alone again, free to restudy materials—and think, think about Louisa Fatio as a person.

One thing I know. Once I'm back at my desk I must do a chronology of the Fleming-Fatio years preceding the start of the novel. Staggering prospect. It is complex!

September 20
9 A.M .

I awoke before first light (even before the St. Augustine trash collectors!) with a somewhat disturbed feeling: I have learned an enormous amount about the genealogy of both families (Fleming and Fatio), about their factual chronology. Lewis Fleming's father, of course, married into the Fatio family soon after he came to Spanish Florida from Ireland in the 1790s. I now know that he married Louisa Fatio's aunt Sophia and that Louisa's young sister, Sophia, is named for her. Study of the family and factual charts made for me by Dena and Hester further indicates the closeness of the two families. Norma Lockwood has even produced a picture of Louisa! (In a way I'm glad none has been found of Margaret herself—only the hint that she closely resembled her father, Charles Seton, Fernandina merchant, much respected, sensitive and genteel. There is a stunning miniature of her father to go by in describing her.) Nothing is known of Margaret's mother, Matilda, and so I'm free to loose my imagination with her. There were several children in the Seton family, but I have just whacked off everyone but Margaret's brother George, who is needed in the plot later on. I know that Indians burned, not one, but two Fatio houses across the river from Hibernia at New Switzerland. I also know that Hibernia houses were burned twice by Seminoles.

The Fatio's spoke six languages, were highly educated and, from having done research for *Maria*, I also know that they were wealthy enough to have chartered their own ship to Florida during the British period. Both Flemings and Fatios received land grants—the Fatios several.

Louisa's grandfather, Francis Philip Fatio, Jr., owned the most extensive library in the region and took a decided interest in young George Fleming soon after his arrival in Florida.

The Fatios are coming clear—but by the time my story opens, I imagine most of them are dead. Louisa and Sophia may be living alone with their servants across the river from Lewis Fleming's Hibernia. I say "may be" because I, at this point, have no idea where I will begin. Louisa Fatio is almost too real to me after my visit to "her house" with Dena. I think I've even "heard" her voice. Too real? Yes. Because I have an uneasy feeling that I have "lost" Margaret. Worse still, perhaps I've never really " had" her. Oh, I know she was small, energetic, sensitive, even beautiful—a woman of deep faith and gigantic courage. But all these were suddenly just words as, this morning, I watched the sky grow gold and then pink from the window of my room.

I am never really settled until I feel I have a straight line to my main character—and with the writing of each new novel I continue to forget that this usually doesn't come until I've found a beginning and an ending. No explanation for that. Simply fact. One thing is sure: I could never write a novel without first knowing the be- ginning and the ending. And so I have set aside this day for Margaret herself— where I will find her first on page 1 and where ultimately I will leave her. Yesterday was Louisa's day. Today, Margaret's.

It is now night. Hour after hour I have read and reread the two privately printed family books— Mrs. Biddle's *Hibernia, The Unreturning Tide and Notes of My Family*, by Susan L'Engle (1888). As I read, I made still another long list of questions and points to discuss with Dena during the next call.

I was still working when evening came—time to meet my friends and book people supreme. Bob and Diana Smith. They have worked wonders for St. Augustine by opening its only complete bookstore, The Booksmith, on the Bay at the north side of the Plaza. At dinner, I sounded them out on the idea of this diary; great reaction, which I value, since they will be selling both this and the novel—to be published simultaneously.

Afterward, I walked slowly back to my motel, alone by choice. Even after a day of thinking and reading, I was still uneasy, still strangely far away from Margaret. A head filling with facts and dates and events, but beyond Louisa Fatio only names. I still had no beginning. If only I could sense (and it is a sensing and one

I usually grope for unsuccessfully several times before I find it) a beginning—where Margaret will be when first you pick up the novel— then I'd know what she'd be doing and why, and I would be moving nearer to the woman herself.

The TV in my room hasn't been on for two days. It was off tonight.

I picked up my current personal reading. *The Letters of William Faulkner.* I put it down again. Got undressed and into a pair of old shorts and a favorite denim work shirt. Not being dressed to be seen in public always lifts my spirit and sharpens my brain.

For several minutes I sat there staring into space, reminding myself that, for me, this mental vacuum, absolutely devoid of plot, comes always at the start of any novel. The confusion does clear, I reminded myself. The ghastly enormities of all those facts and family trees and dates do eventually sort themselves out. The pieces of the puzzle do fit together at last.

I wasn't convinced. Nothing came. The chaos got worse. There would be panic enough and panic often enough once I was free to write. Forget it now. Read. Pick up a book.

I did. But it wasn't Faulkner's letters. Once more it was Mrs. Biddle's *Hibernia.* I read and made notes for two more hours and suddenly—the gift came! So suddenly, in fact, there was no choosing, it was just there. And from nothing I had read in the Biddle book. I "had" my beginning and, glory be, I also " had" Margaret. Oh, I can't quite see her yet, but in the beginning I had just discovered, she was *doing something.* Facing an irrevocable fact. She was in love. And so, she came alive, along with the first concrete evidence of her quite daring nature. The novel will begin with the burial of Augustina, the first wife of Lewis Fleming. Lewis Fleming, the man Margaret hopes to marry.

I rushed to the telephone to do what I always do when something special—good or bad—happens to me. I called by best friend, Joyce Blackburn, with whom I share my home. She is back there in our house in the woods pulling for me to get over these first hurdles. Hurdles she knows well, after seeing me through five such beginnings. And then I called Dena and now here I sit wide-eyed at 11 P.M., trying to get sleepy because I know I'll be up early. (How I wish more desk work, mail, more rewrites on my 1979 title. *Leave Yourself Alone*, and so much time for Christmas were not still up ahead. I long to begin writing about Margaret. But perhaps it's just as well that I can't. The truth is, I am not yet in command of the material. Not yet ready to begin writing— except in my emotions.)

In bed sometime later, the realization came. I reached for this diary and wrote: *Once more, I am embarked on the agonizing, glorious adventure: Trying with all my might to live adequately in two worlds—my own and Margaret Fleming's. In two centuries. Hers and mine. With two sets of friends and relatives. Margaret's and mine. Good luck to me—and to all who will have contact with me!*

September 22
6 A.M.

My last day in St. Augustine for this time. As has been true through the years of coming here for research on *Don Juan McQueen* and *Maria*, a "last day" in St. Augustine is painful. Not because I don't want to go back to my house and island—going home is always good. But there isn't the holiday feeling there. In the midst of so much work? Here? Yes. Each time I leave this little motel room I feel reluctance. I sit (as now) by the window overlooking Matanzas Bay, visible in the soft, Florida sunrise, only half thinking—mostly feeling, experiencing the tiny, ancient city. Early traffic is beginning but not as a city roar—St. Augustine is small, thank heaven. People are going to work and tourists stroll in search of breakfast or out onto the pier where boats of all sizes bob and rock in the quiet water.

Susan Hartridge and Joyce always laughed at Walter, who literally raved about the St. Augustine sky. He would stand (and he stood tall) in front of the Marion Motor Lodge, arms outflung and exclaim about the "high, blue Mediterranean dome." There *is* something different about the St. Augustine sky. Even on a low-clouded, rainy day, the sky remains aloof from the tiny city.

I am still certain about my beginning. That makes me quiet inside. And maybe a little tired. I have worked and worked and worked. That is not only a necessary stage right now, but in a way it prepares me for leaving. There is little more I can do here on this trip. It is all done for now. So, back to St. Simons and very, very different and unrelated work. Oh, I will have to spend at least two days a week reviewing Margaret's material. I dare not "lose" it. I am convinced already that this will be a far more difficult novel to write than *Maria*. It covers a far longer period of time for one thing and Margaret did have all those children! I tend to "lose" children once they're born because I don't know them. That's just another kind of research I'll have to do: Find mothers of different ages who can tell me about children of different ages. Margaret's children were named Seton, Frank, Frederic, William, Matilda, Maggie and Isabel. I wonder what they were like.

October 8
St. Simons Island

During the past two weeks, I have worked at such a wide variety of things, I'm dizzy. First, the inevitable accumulated mail, bills to pay, business to handle which included a trip to see both my attorney, James Gilbert, and Powell Schell, my accountant. (Neither identification is adequate—they are both valued friends.) On September 26, along with telephone calls and letters setting up two interviews, I began the chronology of events which occurred before Margaret's birth and during her childhood. This, not to use in the novel proper, but to familiarize me with her people, her times, the events which shaped her life. This was interrupted only long enough to attend a Policy Committee meeting for our local historical society, my only extracurricular interest these days.

A fresh sorrow: Ruby Wilson, widow of our beloved John Wilson, who took care of us and our house until his death four years ago, had to be rushed back to the hospital for more surgery. Circulatory problems. First a toe was removed, then all her toes, and daily I call or visit her because I love her and because I know it pleases Johnnie that Joyce and I care—as do so many of our friends.

October 2 was my twenty-ninth Spiritual birthday. I became

a Christian on October 2, 1949. Of far more interest to me than June 22, the date I was born. In between watching the baseball playoffs, I continued to work on the complex background chronology, wrote letters, letters and more letters, negotiated a new publishing contract, kept an interview appointment at the Historical Society Museum with Carol Cravey of the publication, *Buckhead Atlanta*—a telephone radio interview, preparatory to a short lecture tour upcoming. First stop is Douglas, Georgia, at the college there on October 10. A date set with a capable book lady named Geneva Womack, who operates the college bookstore. An engagement which has been nearly five years in the making! She and Joyce and I had laughed so much (along with Dianitia Hutcheson, the publicity director at Lippincott) at how long this one has been on the fire that I began to call it the Geneva Conference.

Two days ago I mailed a typescript of my chronology to Dena and Hester for their approval. By long-distance, I have just learned with relief that I'd made very few mistakes in it. Joyce, bless her, will go with me tomorrow on this tour, which moves from Douglas, Georgia, to Columbia, South Carolina, where I will address the South Carolina Library Association's annual meeting.

I'm praying for a reasonably uninterrupted November. I shudder at more diversions which might cause Margaret to dim.

October 17

Home again from the lecture tour and autographing and a providential three-day rest time in a comfortable motel en route to St. Simons from South Carolina, where we did nothing but laugh and read and watch the World Series on a good color TV. (Ours is a small, ancient black and white set which might as well be kept until it stops because we live too far out in the woods to get on the cable.) Being a National League fan, of course, the Series disappointed me, but I loved every minute.

The entire trip, planned too far ahead to cancel simply because the novel was churning in me, turned out to be a wholly creative experience. During the lectures, I was forced to rethink some of my own reasons for writing as I do. What it is I'm really trying to achieve with these books, especially the novels.

As almost always, when I'm asked to speak on writing, I made full and free use of the work of the one author who has influenced me for nearly twenty years—Edmund Fuller, teacher, literary critic for the *Wall Street Journal*, essayist, scholar, novelist—thinker. A thinker with values which match my own. My copy of his long-ago published title *Books With Men Behind Them* (1963) is dog-eared and underlined as no other book I own outside of Pamela Frankau's *Pen to Paper*.

As I move closer to the day when I am free of research and other work to begin writing page 1 of this novel. Fuller's opening lines in *Books With Men Behind Them* fortifies me. (He is using the word "men," of course, in the universal sense. My favorite novelist, the late Gladys Schmitt, is included in his book.) This is the way Edmund Fuller begins it:

> Emerson said, "Talent alone cannot make a writer. There must be a man behind the book." What should be self-evident has become a striking notion in this age of mass publication. Nowadays we tend to reverse the idea and accept somewhat indiscriminately as a writer any man with books behind him. The man behind the book . . . clearly is required to have something more than talent. One of the troubles of a glibly articulate time is that talent is extolled by itself, and sometimes no other qualifying appraisal is made. Many a wretched book has been foisted upon us on the dubious plea that the writer had talent.

To some, this may seem as though Fuller is saying that the measure of a writer's talent is relatively unimportant, or that the writer should be some manner of superior person in order to bring " enough" to his or her book. I readily admit that Edmund Fuller is the only living writer whom I've longed to meet. I never shall most likely, and so I don't attempt to explain his book, but of this much I am certain: Writers ought to be talented in the use of words. This should go without saying. As Mr. Fuller says, "... talent should be taken for granted as the minimal technical equipment necessary to get into print." But once the book is into print, then what?

One of my favorite chapters in Fuller's book is The Post-Chatterley Deluge. After all the hubbub—legal and otherwise—following the availability in the fifties of *Lady Chatterley's Lover* (not Lawrence's best book by any means, but the most sexually titillating), we were indeed "deluged" with similar "literary" efforts, so that both publishers and authors could begin thinking in six figures. With Mr. Fuller, I deplore even the thought of censorship. It must never happen in America. But also with him, I deplore the fact that most books have to be pre-read before they are freely given as gifts in order to avoid shocking or repelling.

Someday, perhaps. I'll meet someone who knows Fuller and can tell me what manner of man he really is. Is he a Christian believer? I would think so. Is he a—prude? I am sure not. He strikes me as being a man of taste and values and humor and love and faith. Of course, I quoted him in both Douglas, Georgia, at South Georgia College, and to the librarians in South Carolina. I noticed that when I mentioned his chapter on the " post-Chatterley deluge" only those near my own age laughed. The younger librarians seemed not to get my point. But I was not lecturing against so-called dirty books. Nor was I crusading (I have never!) for so-called clean books. I've seen many in the latter category which reek as literature and this does no one, particularly God, any credit.

Talent *should* "be taken for granted as the minimal technical equipment necessary to get into print." What talent I have is, I believe, a direct gift from God and I have no delusions that He was overly generous with me. But what I have, I attempt to sharpen and hone to its limits. And what I bring to a book is entirely my responsibility. Furthermore, the reader is, in whatever way I may influence him, also my responsibility.

As nearly as I now see it, the theme of Margaret Fleming's story will be "the obligation to hope." I do not preach religious values when I write fiction (no one should) but I do attempt to put something into every book that stimulates—hope.

Tragedy permeates life and so most stories based on fact, as are my novels so far, contain much tragedy. And yet, I will wait and wait and work and work—and even pray—to find a way to leave the reader with at least something to hope for. Certain recent novels I have read leave me feeling as though I ought at least to consider suicide!

This is some of what I spoke about on this brief lecture tour—and " lecture" is the wrong word. I simply talk. Without notes. But I do think it out ahead of time, so, as I now recall, these were the things I said I attempted to do with every novel I write:

1. I try to give my readers usually needed escape (healthy escape is good for us all) from their monotonous or hectic or troubled lives. I try first of all to tell a good story.

2. Since the average person won't read history books, I spend every effort, every dollar and day I can afford making certain that my history is accurate. I believe a knowledge of history past gives us perspective and courage for the history we're living through today.

3. I am a believer in Jesus Christ; since I would be bored to write a book which did not include Him, I attempt sincerely to show His divine intervention and involvement with all human life. Not Christian doctrine—divine involvement.

4. Finally, I attempt to affirm beauty. Hope. In some often fragile, but nonetheless real, sense a novelist can point the way back to the Garden.

I'm glad I did some fresh "affirming" for myself during the trip by being forced to communicate my beliefs, because when Joyce and I returned home, four traumas awaited me: Mother had been rushed to the hospital; the first letter on the stack of waiting mail told of the death of the husband of one of my favorite people, Marion Conner of Jacksonville, who performs with such artistry one-woman dramatic monologues of entire novels— mine and others; the second letter brought news of the impending death of the husband of my dear friend from college days, Eleanor Ratelle, of the Miami *Herald*. The fourth trauma was not tragic—but traumatic nonetheless: The septic tank stopped up the first hour we were home!

October 18

Worked from a little after dawn until evening at my desk, trying between duties all day long to reach Marion Conner by long-distance. For years. I've been aware of my deep feelings for her as an artist and as a human being, but her sudden tragedy— dear John's death—is strangely my own. I must make contact with her. And I would certainly understand, since they all deal with grief and sorrow, if Marion could never give another of her beautiful performances of even one of my novels. Especially *Maria*, whose David died as suddenly as did Marion's John.

Later

I reached Marion at last. All the world's tears were in her voice, but with strength and reassurance for me. "Please don't worry about me, Genie. I leave tomorrow for Jesup, Georgia, to do *Maria* and then I drive to Valdosta to repeat it. I am trying to think of only one thing—to make them the best performances of your *Maria* I've ever done!"

I sat for a long time after we hung up, marveling at the greatness of a human spirit linked to God.

October 20

I am still quiet and somehow girded by Marion's strength in spite of frequent long-distance calls to and from Mother's hospital room in Charleston, West Virginia. Thank God for Nancy Goshorn, my friend—closer than a sister—who cares for Mother for love's sake. Nancy, who knows Marion, is fortified by her courage, too. My novel *Maria* is dedicated to Nancy. I wish she knew how true it is that with Mother so ill the slim grasp I now have on the new novel would already be gone were Nancy not there—as she is.

I was up early this morning, hoping to handle some complex business matters, call about Mother and write eleven or twelve letters before noon. I made it by 2 P.M., and now, for the remainder of the day, I must write a new Foreword for my old book *Beloved World*, which Zondervan Publishing House is bringing out in 1979 in a new anniversary edition. Nineteen seventy-nine marks my twenty-fifth year as a published author.

Ruby Wilson is home from the hospital, but for how long, no one knows.

October 22

Little will be written this week in these pages. The days are filled with work, but the kind of work that makes altogether uninteresting reading. Every day I try—I don't always make it but I try—to spend some time with Margaret: reading something, almost anything that will keep her in my mind through the final stages of checking type-script on my 1979 book. *Leave Yourself Alone*, plus business, business (much still unsettled and cloudy, although important where my writing future is concerned) and calls, calls, calls; blurbs for other authors' books, a few interviews, and so on.

Two happy prospects for October 25: Mother will go home from the hospital, and my valued and much loved Zondervan editor, Judy Markham, is flying down to the Island. She will bring along Carol Holquist (someone I'm sure to like), who has just been made director of author relations at Zondervan. More publishing houses should create such a position.

October 27

Our time with Judy and Carol was about 10 percent more fun and more profitable than even Joyce and I had supposed it would be. We love them both so much and I'm truly pleased that Zondervan, which has published most of my religious titles, will make something of my twenty-fifth anniversary in 1979. Friendships there have lasted sturdily through all those years. Zondervan published my first book in 1954. A little opus called *Discoveries*.

With every joy (at my age) comes another sadness. Mother is better, but dear Ruby Wilson went back in the hospital today. We fear her leg will be amputated this time.

October 30

Up early to do the few rewrites and additions Judy Markham suggested for my manuscript of *Leave Yourself Alone*. I wonder how much I'm leaving myself alone? How much I'm practicing what I preach? I am trying, but there are so many (more than mentioned here) pressures and sorrows, some days flowing like a river. As they flow, at times, into every life. Mine is certainly no different, but any craftsman worth his or her hire keeps the tools sharp and if I don't do something soon to break this flood of diversions from the novel, I will be in trouble. How I wish I could think of a title . . .

Later

Enjoyed the day working on Judy's suggestions for *Leave Yourself Alone*. They vastly improve the manuscript of the book which I expect will go on helping its author keep her perspective for years to come. Haven't quite decided how to break the "down" pattern of interruptions and problems, but I must do something. Very tired.

November 3
St. Augustine, Florida

Decision made: Go to St. Augustine! I am here and, as always, elevated in my spirit in the first hour! I drove the hundred miles down alone again, thanking God all the way that Dena and Hester are so involved with me in the novel. What would I do without them? I took a new route—forsaking my favorite A-iA through Fernandina. I drove I-95 south from Brunswick to 295 and over the breathtaking St. Johns River on a long, long high bridge which gave me a view of the river from the Fatio- New

Switzerland side across to Fleming's Hibernia. I took this route deliberately, for Margaret's sake. The old route is still *Don Juan McQueen* and *Maria* to me. Heaven knows, there are enough pressures in my business and personal life so that whatever small hand-up I can give myself will add to the new novel. Even a thing so small as a route change. Tiredness, the need for an unattainable rest period, and the ongoing pressures make concentration difficult. And so I am here in order to narrow my choices. In St. Augustine, there is for me no choice but to work on the novel in progress. At my desk on the Island, I fell apart in the face of all the choices there. Dena is coming and she is still enough of the fine teacher she once was to keep me on my toes preparing for her arrival. She arrives tomorrow and her "student" has no choice but to cram today!

November 4

Up at 6 A.M. I have studied genealogies galore, the Civil War in north Florida from an outline Dena made, also her expert rundown of the 1835 portion of the Second Seminole War (and *only* she could "run it down" so succinctly). I have studied steamboats on the St. Johns, the route from the St. Johns into St. Augustine, and now I will once more go over the background chronology *and* by some means find the courage to face that formidable folder of maps! Many people love maps. I detest them, but they are essential. Knowing where you are and how to get there is basic to life—and to writing a novel.

November 7

Dena has come and gone and I miss her. One doesn't miss a dim light which has been turned off, but a bright one is different. She is, for me, a bright, bright light. I continue to marvel at her sensitivity to me, her skills, her imaginative approach to my needs as a novelist, her connections, her charm, and her altogether enjoyable zaniness. If, ideally, I could block out all of life except Dena, Hester, my folders and this book, the novel could be done in one-third the time it will undoubtedly take. (Time, of course, is one of my horrendous pressures right now. I have succumbed for many reasons to a publisher's deadline of one short year and a half for both this diary and the novel.)

I considered not writing the following, but decided it should be here since an author's physical condition is as integral a part of writing a novel as anything else. A year ago I was ill for nearly two months with, as I understand it, an imbalance of the fluid in the middle ear. Being an optimist by nature, I didn't expect it to return: the nausea, the dizziness, the always unexpected blitzes of sliding ceilings and walls and bookshelves. Surely, it is not as severe an attack of the stuff this time, but on Dena's first morning here, I awakened (was awakened) at four-thirty with a "blitz." I grabbed my head and sat on the side of the motel bed refusing it for a minute or so. And then, I accepted. If it turned out to follow last year's pattern, I would be at least periodically wretched for two months or so.

Dena was great. She'd had one or two sieges of it too in her life and so remained cheerful but saw to it that I slept sitting bolt upright in the bed, made no quick movements, and so on. She also insisted upon doing the driving for our much anticipated expedition to Hibernia to see the interior of St. Margaret's, the little Episcopal church which Margaret built (named not for her but for a saint), to meet the Reverend Mr. Bob Libby, the rector, to see Fleming descendant Hester Williams and Ximenez-Fatio house researcher Norma Lockwood again; and to be taken through the present house, near the site of old Hibernia, constructed of many of its materials. Not once did I consider not going through with our day. So we started out in Dena's Pacer and, in spite of the sickening, full-empty-light-heavy head I carried, it was glorious!

A few minutes before the appointed time of 10 A.M. we drew up in front of Margaret's charming clapboard church beside the narrow, winding sand road that flows off a busy, four-laned highway, back under giant oaks and into the nineteenth century. Hester Williams was already there from Jacksonville, with Norma Lockwood, Jane Rowley (Margaret Fleming's great-granddaughter), and Mrs. Kathleen McKee (who lives across the road from the church and whom I'd met and liked on the first visit Joyce and I made there months ago). Everyone wanted to wait for Bob Libby before I caught my first glimpse of the interior of the quaint little church that had been my Margaret's dream. So we wandered under the big oaks and magnolias behind the church to the cemetery, where I made a sketch on a card of what could turn out to be the setting for Scene 1, Chapter 2, Or, perhaps, a Prologue.

Whirling head and all, I was on cloud nine. And amazed that each member of our party appeared to be as excited as I that a novel about Margaret Seton Fleming was about to begin. Not in a hundred years could I adequately express my wonder and gratitude at the shared enthusiasm I'm enjoying already from those who still care deeply about Margaret and her church at Hibernia.

Stepping inside the chapel is an experience. Most of the others were already familiar with it from Sunday attendance, but sensitive to my moment, they, too, were hushed. Long and narrow, the tiny building, its dark-stained wood-paneled walls and ceiling seemed to shut in the moment and hold it suspended. "It seats sixty—thin," Hester declared. The dark-stained altar is simple, its slender cross, plain gold, but the stained-glass windows are among the loveliest I've seen anywhere. One, depicting an orange grove, Hester doesn't like—"Whoever saw oranges *that* orange?"—but Margaret's window, deep, glowing blue, green and ruby, set high behind the altar and filling the end of the church, is just right for Margaret as I've already come to know her.

The church itself, I learned that day, was begun as Margaret could afford materials and labor, sometime in the mid-1870's, with work done at irregular intervals until its completion in 1882, almost five years after her death. In fact, in her final illness, work had resumed so that she could lie in her bed and listen to the builders at work. Actually, the first service held in the little church was Margaret's funeral, but the building was far from completed. Chairs had to be brought from her house for the service, since church pews were still a long way off.

After a time, we left the chapel, I with no reluctance, because I knew I'd be back often during the writing of the novel.

After an affectionate good-bye to Kathleen McKee and Jane Rowley, I was warmly greeted—along with Hester, Dena, Norma and Bob Libby—by hospitable Nancy Morris, who now lives in a house built about 1956 near the site of old Hibernia. Nancy not only did me the honor of telling me that she had read my nonfiction titles through the years, she urged me to absorb to my heart's content everything—the wood, the glass, the bricks—which had been in Margaret's house and reused in the present one. I reveled in actually being able to touch the railing that Margaret had touched when the old stair-case had been a part of her Hibernia. Termites had made restoration impossible, but the seven massive, tall chimneys of Margaret's enormous home had contained enough bricks to build the entire new house. I knew Margaret and Lewis Fleming had built a thirty-roomed house, but until I saw the size of Nancy Morris's home, built entirely from its chimneys, I had not yet dreamed the old place as large as it must have been.

From the Morris home we walked the sun-slashed riverbank and tried to imagine exactly where Margaret's promenade had been over which her paying guests from the North had strolled during their sojourns at Hibernia in the days preceding and following the Civil War. Dena and I felt certain we knew exactly where her double row of crepe myrtles had stood. The long pier (seven hundred feet) is there, many of the largest trees are surely the same, and in less than an hour, I felt I was ready to write scenes laid outside under the trees beside the wide, wide St. Johns.

Luncheon in Orange Park with Hester, Norma, Dena and Bob was (again, in spite of my funny head) animated. I think the food was excellent too, but it did not have my attention. This was Bob Libby's first exposure to a novelist at work on large and small details and he sat grinning in amazement at the concentration and careful detail given by Dena, Norma, Hester and me to the puzzle of what kind of "fancy clock" might have been mentioned in the inventory of Margaret's possessions left in the house at her death. We knew there was a dining room cuckoo clock— it was left to a son in her will. But the "fancy clock" was found at the time of the inventory in her bedroom. Finally, after about twenty minutes of our hashing and rehashing a probable description of her bedroom clock for possible use in a future scene. Bob Libby interrrupted: "I can't sit here in silence any longer without telling you, Genie, that I am dumbfounded at all the picky-picky detail you go into to do one of these books!" Of course, his women friends at the table laughed, looked and felt a bit smug at our "professionalism" and the meal went on. It ended with Bob Libby moving to my end of the long table, where we held a one-to-one brief but potent conversation about Jesus Christ and some of my books of Christian apologetics. (That word has always bothered me—*apologetics*?) Bob and I ended our talk with my promise that he could interview me early in 1979 for an article to appear in the *National Episcopalian*.

For me the day was crowded with joy. Joy with vertigo? You bet. Especially the remainder of the concentrated talk at the restaurant as Dena hit Hester and Norma with one after another of her questions jotted down during our ten-hour work session the day before. I see no way to begin much actual writing until the new year, but at least Margaret is "back" and, dizzy or not, I am once again focused.

November 8

Dena, bless her, delivered me to my motel yesterday, then left for Jacksonville. Up early again to check on election returns, also to sit over coffee in my room—just being, and allowing my mind to roam over many things. My head is still troublesome, but I refuse to cancel an anticipated visit at noon from my longtime college friend Edith Cowles, who will drive down from Orange Park. I need to talk about the kind of things Edith and I share. At Ohio University, back in the thirties, she was my dormitory "literary idol." The Edna St. Vincent Millay of Lindley Hall. No contact for years and years and, now, good contact again. The best kind. We share the excitement not only of our love of writing—but of Jesus Christ as well. *And* Margaret! Edith has just become a communicant of Margaret's little church at Hibernia.

Later

The time with Edith was beautiful. I long for more such leisurely conversations. I need them. And yet they cannot be sought out or arranged. Such times of seeing myself today against the perspective of the years, of seeing Edith today against the perspective of the same years—these times are gifts. From the One who has made us *one*. I felt free to talk to Edith, as I most certainly did, of my innermost goals for the kinds of books I write. As did Joyce, Dena, Hester, Norma and Bob Libby, Edith responded positively to my proposed theme—*the obligation to hope*.

I believe there is still time to walk to the Historical Society Library and listen to a tape Jackie Bearden has concerning the events surrounding the surrender of St. Augustine to the Yankees on March 9, 1862. I leave for home tomorrow before noon. Hope my head is clear enough to drive.

November 9

Again, as always, a somewhat sad day. The familiar reluctance takes over. I love this little city, but it is more than that. Here, I am free to concentrate only on writing. Joyce and my home up the road—waiting—cheer me, though, as I get ready to head back to dailiness. What will it be like, I wonder, when I'm working in another area of the U.S.? Perhaps not even along the southern coast. I can't go on writing novels about this area until I'm eighty-two, and I fully expect to be doing them at least another twenty years. Preferably longer.

My head is still not good (Pray God, that I have no more of those sudden blitzes!), but I can drive and I am *not* depressed by the attacks. I've worked like a Trojan (how hard *did* Trojans work?) since I've been here, but I have been rested by it. There are no conflicts, no pressures here in St. Augustine. Today, somehow, I understand more about what I mean by our *obligation to hope*. There will be pressures, new problems, old ones still there, once I'm back where I can be contacted at my desk. Will I be ready? I believe so. I loathe problems as much as anyone else. Beyond my faith, I have no answers.

There are none. I dread going back. I also welcome it. It will give me a chance to learn a little better how to cope while not feeling well. I am not being dramatic about what I might find.

Merely realistic. My dear Ruby Wilson is back in the hospital—this time undoubtedly for further amputation. Her suffering these past months is part of the load I carry. As it is with anyone who loves and watches suffering. Mother's suffering is past for now. I am grateful. I am grateful for so much.

November 10
Still in St. Augustine

Joyce, also a writer, came, again, to my rescue. From the sound of my weary voice on long-distance just before I was to leave yesterday, she could tell that I needed—especially for my dizzy head—another day or so away from work. She and Elsie Goodwillie, not only our valued manuscript typist for as long as we've lived on St. Simons Island but one of our closest friends, got right in Joyce's car and are now driving down to see to it that I relax for a few days and have some fun. "That may clear your head and you'll feel better more quickly than if you push to get on with the work."

I feel as though I've been handed a reprieve!

November 14
St. Augustine

It makes me a little ill even to write this, but it is fact: Early this morning, still in bed, I had another attack of that buzzy vertigo!

This afternoon (our last day here) we drove across the St. Johns from Green Cove Springs and found the side road to New Switzerland, the site of the old Fatio plantation, which stood almost directly across the river from Hibernia. For weeks, we have been searching the records for Louisa Fatio's burial place. In her will she requested that she be buried "in the little cemetery near St. Augustine." Well, there are a lot of "little cemeteries," but she must be, we've concluded, in the Fatio family plot near their old home at New Switzerland, now so over-grown with dense Florida woods as to be lost. New Switzerland is less than a half-hour's drive from the city. One would think, though, that Louisa would have specified New Switzerland. There are always conjectures.

Did we drive past her grave today? Almost certainly.

How I long to be able to talk through this novel—my budding plans for it— with Tay. But she is gone.

November 23
Thanksgiving Day
on St. Simons Island

The reader who knows my *St. Simons Memoir* knows my beloved 102-year-old friend, Lorah Plemmons, who only left us a short time ago. Well, her twin daughters, Sarah and Mary, are carrying on in her generous tradition: Before they left for New England last fall, they prepared and froze a complete Thanksgiving dinner for us. All we supplied was the cranberry sauce! No one cooks a turkey as Sarah does; so, to celebrate our happy windfall, we invited Elsie and Dena to share it with us. Dena drove up from Jacksonville about midmorning, and, of course, we talked nonstop about Margaret's story.

The Island is at its sunniest best at this time of year, the day was as nearly perfect as a day can be. In all ways. Oh, my head was horrible (both full and empty at once!). But I don't recall a happier Thanksgiving. I am blessed. So many people give to me in so many ways.

November 27

Long days of inching forward on the novel chronology. History books, pages turned down and marked with black pencil, are strewn across my office. For me a chronology of a novel has to do with listing both family and historical events by years—the years covered in the book. Dull to record here, except to say I am alternately high and low and working hard—still with the vertigo. It is almost like a possessive friend by now.

November 28

Joe and Fifi Lippincott (Joe is Chairman of the Board of the J. B. Lippincott Company, my longtime publisher) are on the Island today and are taking Joyce and me to lunch. It is nearing time for Joe to retire and, although I am not often what is recognizable as "nervous," today I am. Of course, part of my anxiety is the increasingly desperate need for uninterrupted time. The upcoming Christmas holidays will take me away from the Island and once more stop the process, however happily. (Here indeed is the perfect example of the difficulty of living in two centuries at once.) I leave December 13 to spend Christmas with Mother. Workdays are running out. But I am also jittery about being with Joe and Fifi, for fear Joe will tell me that he is, indeed, retiring. He has been a part of the Lippincott family from the beginning of my long association there. Almost everyone else I knew during those early years is gone for one reason or another now. At least Joe and Fifi will go on being our friends.

If I don't finish the chronology, or at least a few pages of Chapter 1 before I leave December 13, getting back into it will be that much more difficult in January.

"Doesn't an author just sit down and write?" Not on your tintype!

November 29

Two things have lifted my spirit and I am whaling away (papers and books spread everywhere!) on the chronology. First, a gorgeous bouquet of fall flowers from my new, sensitive Macon friend, Jimmie Harnsberger, and the time spent yesterday with Joe and Fifi. Both are more meaningful than I can explain here.

Joe Lippincott, by the way, urged me to write more in the pages of this diary about what it means to work out a novel chronology. I argued with him a little—it seemed too complicated. But, I'm sure he's right. Here I copy my chronology, as scribbled, for the opening years of the story: 1832, 1833, 1834, 1835.

1832 — Begin at Augustina Fleming's funeral service in the Hibernia cemetery. Margaret admits to Louisa Fatio her dream of marrying Lewis Fleming. She can wait, if necessary, until she is an old woman. Andrew Jackson is president. His Indian policy would relocate all Indians west of the Mississippi. Lewis Fleming must know all about this. Jackson-ville, founded in 1822 and named for Andrew Jackson, then governor of the Florida Territory, and incorporated in 1832. Find a way to get in family and history background (with a light hand) via Lewis Fleming teaching his two sons, George and L. I.

1833 — Margaret Seton must visit the Fatios'— first, small moves toward getting Margaret and Lewis together. Teaching goes on, mainly history.

1834 — Be sure you get in Indian background in Lewis's teaching sessions with his sons. Also, his ongoing grief over his beautiful Spanish wife, Augustina.

1835 — There is a hard freeze at Hibernia. Complete loss of orange groves. Lewis, a major in the Florida Militia, will be called soon to fight Seminoles. Build via his commanding officer. Colonel Warren, in Jacksonville. He is called. He fights in Battle of Withlacoochee, December 31, 1835, and is severely wounded in the leg. (Watch turn of the new year, 1836. It is here that Indians burn both Hibernia and the Fatio house at New Switzerland—with Fleming children and Margaret Seton visiting there for Christmas, and Lewis gone.)

Enough. Year by year, a chronology moves ahead, with national events which parallel family events lined up as a skeleton for building the novel's suspense and story. I must be as familiar with events as though I lived then. As of now, handling the ultimate romance, about which Lewis knows nothing at this point, could prove difficult. Hard to make believable. But that is not for today. Today, the chronology has moved only to the year 1860, in which I must begin rumblings of the Civil War and prepare the way for the first of Margaret's tragic losses.

The truth is, once the writing is underway, the characters themselves will begin to take over. I welcome this. The only way I attempt to keep them in check is by cracking the whip of my determination that all actual facts be authentic.

November 30

Another slight "middle ear syndrome" attack this A.M. I feel lousy, but I have a luncheon date and errands (Christmas shopping, such as it is), so I'm going to ignore my head (since I won't be using it) and go ahead with the day's schedule as planned. Tomorrow, surely, back to the chronology. I have an autographing party coming up on December 2 at Island Bookshelf here on St. Simons. Must stop by there today, too, as well as sign books at two other stores. This will be a day of getting things be- hind me. (And a month from now, this entire entry will sound like much ado about nothing!)

December 3

Yesterday, a most successful, busy party at Island Book- shelf with the happy surprise of the arrival of Jimmie Harnsberger and friends (who drove all the way from Macon for the ten minutes we managed together!). A good day, but until almost time to dress, I was totally unaware of *how* I was going to make it. Head again. Signing and then looking up to speak with the people who came to buy books sent my head into a loony limbo. We all laughed—what else was there to do when I had to ask each one to wait a minute, until *he* or *she* stopped going in circles!

Today, I am no better and trying to be positive about tomorrow. At work on the chronology again, but it may be all out of whack. One incident—frustrating and also funny—comes to mind from the autographing party yesterday: A bouncy lady asked: " Don't you have another novel about ready for me to buy? It's been such a long time! You aren't getting lazy, are you?" I hope I made a sane response. All I managed that I remember, was another laugh. It helped.

December 5

Two more days of dizzies, not severe except for the first two hours out of bed in the morning. I get up early to be ready to work eventually. The chronology creeps along, today was desk clearing—mail, mail—etc., until now at 4 P.M., head dizzy, just when it's time to bathe and dress for a birthday dinner party for my longtime friend Agnes Holt, I am suddenly "possessed" by the urge to begin writing Chapter 1! Just put aside the chronology until I feel better and write.

Perverse?

Perverse.

At the beginning of this day, " dizzily" reading Proverbs, I felt a peculiar sense of elation. Nothing of a spiritual "high." (I am always wary of those so-called emotional highs or "anointings," since I firmly believe God is *always* attempting to give to us.) What happened to me had to do with facing the obvious fact (to which I had been blinded by stacks of duties and problems) that I needed to stop research and begin to write. Even if I toss it all away.

For the entire year (and Joyce agrees) I have fallen into an emotional bind of overconscientiousness—in answering mail, paying bills, handling business, visiting the sick, calling the sorrowful, and being available when I didn't have any business being! Can a Christian *not* be available? No. Within reason, we must be, no matter the cost to us. But Christians, as well as anyone else, can go overboard. I had gone *way* overboard. In my frantic attempt to get things done in order to get to writing, I answered letters too promptly (which usually meant replies to my replies almost by return mail and in no time there I sat with the stack as high as ever!). I had allowed certain people to become too accustomed to a regular call from me and so on. I can't even remember what in Proverbs showed me this today, but I am shown! And, to free myself and regain some sanity, I am putting the unfinished chronology back in its folder and letting the mail stack up. I am going to write something besides dates and events, checks, and letters! Since my doctor believes the vertigo is caused by stress. I'm going to be good to me. *I'm going to write Scene 1 of Chapter 1 tomorrow.*

Undoubtedly all this sounds far out. For me, it is liberation. I have spent the year "accomplishing," being responsible—I thought. The muse, however limited my modest talent, is a wild woman at times. And glad I am that, at sixty-two, I can still respond to her demands. I am in joyful rebellion against being a responsible drudge!

I am going to write tomorrow.

Margaret Seton Fleming will, however feebly, begin to live and breathe again if I live until I get to my type-writer tomorrow!

December 6

Why did I wait so long to do this?

Six pages down now. Not very good, dialogue overdone and some facts need more study. But Margaret has spoken her first few lines on paper and I will sleep tonight.

December 9

Two more days spent on playing around with Scene 1, Chapter 1. Or is it a Prologue? The playing around has ended for now. Only time to finish shopping and errands and pack to leave for Mother's house on December 13. My head is rotten.

December 10

I find what I am about to write almost unbelievable. A letter that arrived yesterday from Dr. Howard Gotlieb, curator of my papers at Boston University, informed me that Edmund Fuller and his wife, Ann, would be on St. Simons during Christmas!

My heart leaped and then sank. I'd be away—at home with Mother, Nancy and her aunt, Mary Jane, for Christmas. I called Howard at once. He promised to get in touch with Edmund Fuller and write to me at Mother's house. At least he held out hope that maybe, just maybe, the Fullers might be staying on the Island until my return, December 29. I can think of nothing that would mean more to me right now than a chance actually to converse with the author and critic who has reinforced my thinking about books for so many years.

December 11

Middle ear syndrome wears itself out, the doctors say. May it be soon. Yesterday evening, I could do no more than sit and watch Joyce decorate our living room which, of course, because she goes to her mother too, will be empty on Christmas day. We had our first fire in the fireplace and turned on the record player, and Vivaldi and Bach and Joyce and I were together. There is at least a chance that I may meet Edmund Fuller. And a new year is coming.

I have an "obligation to hope." I *am* hopeful.

December 29

Back again on my island after Christmas and a five-and-a-half-hour wait each way between planes in Atlanta. Joyce is still away. The Plemmons sisters, Mary and Sarah, and Elsie Goodwillie met my plane at 8 P.M. It is late. My head is still bad—goofy—and I am tired. But I long to attempt here to put down at least some of the gratitude I feel to the friends who met me, fed me, brought me home, carried in my baggage—and to Nancy Goshorn and Mother and Mary Jane (who combined forces to do so much to give me true TLC during the Christmas holidays). Mother's beautiful house was quiet, the weather moderate, the meaning of Christmas deepened by the love all three showed me—and I *slept*. Slept and slept and slept.

My time there was quiet and deep and filled with joy. Can one know joy with nearly perpetual vertigo? Yes. The joy of loving, of being loved—and of needed rest.

Joy? I'm trying to contain it this minute, in spite of the way I feel physically, because while I was at Mother's, a letter came from Dr. Howard Gotlieb of Boston University telling me that I will, after all, meet with Edmund Fuller. He is still on the Island and will call me tomorrow.

December 30

I opened mail—for seven hours. Most of it continued the same outpouring of love I received at Mother's. Three letters contained more tragic news. Deaths to shatter the lives of three people whom I love. I am not one of those persons who stays in touch with a lot of college friends. Two of the few: Edith Cowles and Eleanor (Diz) Ratelle, of the Miami *Herald*. Eleanor's gentle husband died while I was away, and Marion Conner's sister-in-law (how magnificently Marion will interpret Margaret Fleming someday!). Death came also into the life of our closest and dearest writer friend, Vinnie Williams. Her husband. I made contact with all three and then I called Ruby Wilson, who, while I was gone, lost her leg.

I will spend tomorrow morning making some small dent in the mountain of Christmas mail and will also make a conscious effort to remain close to God, who alone can cope with both shared grief and joy at the same instant.

I need to know how to contain both because Mr. Fuller called and *I will* see him and his wife, Ann, here at my house this afternoon. For this author with the whirling head—*joy*.

January 1, 1979
New Year's Day

I am alone in my house in the woods as I am so often on the first day of a new year. I rather like it. Southerners eat ham hocks and black-eyed peas on New Year's for luck, Yankees eat cabbage (and my grandmother always cooked a dime in it!). I write. Superstition does not rule my life, but it is said that whatever one does on New Year's Day one will do all year. And so, since I care so little about doing anything else (aside from reading), I write.

It is a soft Island winter day with sunshine picking out the trunks of my old oak trees, and I am still experiencing the glow of the time spent with Edmund and Ann Fuller. To write of the deep significance of their visit would not only embarrass them but overtax my talent. Of course—of course, Edmund's talk of books, his strong concern for eroding values in literature again reinforced mine. I will have to confess to feeling honored that he had read two of my novels: *Don Juan McQueen* and my first. *The Beloved Invader.* He seemed to consider the reading time well spent. My head was bad during the visit, but my heart quiet. Like me, he has been criticized for writing of Christian values. Of expressing in the words I will give to Margaret Fleming—the "obligation to hope."

Nasty reviews have happily not bothered me much during my long writing life (and, naturally. I've had them), but now I doubt that they will faze me at all. Any author longs to have his or her words read and liked, but all readers cannot like all books, and although Edmund Fuller is a far finer craftsman than I, at least we share some of the same nasty criticism. We have the "right literary enemies." How God must enjoy the faith of such a fine intellect and such a warmhearted, delightful gentleman! How God must enjoy everything there is to enjoy about his attractive, supportive, intelligent wife, Ann.

Edmund (and we were all three on a first-name basis at once) signed my well-read old copy of his fine *Books With Men Behind Them*. He seemed extraordinarily pleased that I had liked that particular title for so many years. Accompanied by their two dogs, the Fullers are working on a new southern research project. May their research bring them back to St. Simons Island sooner than they expect!

When we bid one another good-bye, Edmund said: " Genie, we have established a friendship." And so we have.

I will read for the remainder of this New Year's Day. My variety of reading fare amuses me. In the past month I've read a startlingly well-done first novel by Brenda Peterson called *A River of Light*; a new book. *The Awakening of St. Augustine*, by Robert Graham, *James Jones: A Friendship*, by Willie Morris, and am well into Arthur Schlesinger's biography of Robert Kennedy. I am a bookaholic. If there isn't a stack of unread books waiting on the corner of my desk, I grow jittery. There are six new ones now—a glorious feast for the New Year. I've been "into" Virginia Woolf's thick volumes of diaries and letters all year and Joyce gave me a new one for Christmas. Hurray!

January 3

For two days I have rewritten my scribbles done during the last days of 1978 for this diary. An interesting way to start a new year—with an immediate perspective on the ending of the old. Some days I feel sure my vertigo is gone. Today, I wonder. But Joyce is en route home in her little Oldsmobile Cutlass, and a new year has begun. As always, I am stimulated by the prospect, although I try every morning to remember that, as my maternal grandmother used to say, "Each day is a day made new."

Best of all this time, the new year contains for me an- other novel. Right now, I am both far away from Margaret Fleming and her story and exhilarated by the thought of it.

January 7

For four days I've been neck-deep in assembling IRS materials, trying to understand and fill in the right amounts for numerous forms covering the three friends who work for me—my "enormous" payroll. And I have been, of course, answering letters. One after another after another. (An English friend, Kathleen Chambers, wrote recently: "Answering mail in bulk must be a horrendous project." I love her use of the word *bulk*. True.) They were almost all warm and encouraging letters, though, and now, with the event upcoming today, I am as near exhilaration as I've been in weeks. The event? The arrival of our longtime friend to whom I've dedicated my book *Leave Yourself Alone*—Frances Pitts, of Duluth, Minnesota.

Frances comes to the Island every winter and although my schedule prevents our seeing enough of each other, it helps me just knowing she's here. The reason? She is one of my most effective encouragers and a true book enthusiast. Every telephone conversation with her all winter and every meeting will stimulate me to work harder. She has the delightful ability to "live through" the writing of every book with both Joyce and me. Why it helps so much, I can't fully explain.

With Elsie Goodwillie, we'll meet Frances's plane, have dinner at Elsie's house and then settle Frances into her favorite motel room at Queen's Court.

January 9

A Prologue has now been toyed with and rewritten several times. I've lost count. I still tend toward a Prologue instead of making the material in it Chapter 1, because I want that particular block of story to stand alone. It sets the movement for the entire book. Now I'm facing squarely the absolute necessity of completing that detailed chronology. Confession: I have been stalling on this because my head has just not been up to it.

Nothing about writing one of these historical novels is as brain-bending (for me, at least) as doing a year-by-year chronology of births, deaths, national, world and local events. I loathe it. But the time has come.

January 10

Chronology all day, nine to nearly five. And, unless I can handle the discovered gaps in information long-distance with Dena, I am relieved and delighted that another trip to St. Augustine is in the offing. Am I delighted because I love going so much? Yes. Am I delighted because it will give me a legitimate excuse to postpone the remainder of this difficult task of untangling the chronology? Yes.

January 11

Dena, bless her, will meet me in St. Augustine at noon, Monday, January 15, and stay with me until January 17. She will also arrange for us to drive to Hibernia on the St. Johns so that I may visit and talk with Mrs. Dorothy Austin, granddaughter of Margaret Fleming. Mrs. Austin, mother of Jane Rowley, who was so helpful the day I first saw the inside of Margaret's little church, should be able to fill in some of my information gaps. At any rate, she seems pleased that I'm doing the story and I'm grateful for her time. I hope Jane is there, too. I liked her very much.

For the remainder of today (I leave tomorrow for two days of study preparatory to Dena's arrival), Joyce and I will do errands in Brunswick: Take our IRS material to the firm of Schell and Hogan so our wonderful Beth Edwards there can keep us on good terms with the U.S. government; go to the Glynn County Courthouse for our car tags; and shop. Practical Islanders tend to try to accomplish as much as possible when a trip across the salt creeks and marshes is necessary. This is nothing against Brunswick; the old part of the city is a delight. My reason to get everything done at once has to do with the fact that I am perfectly content to stay inside my own gate for weeks at a time. When forced to emerge, I do it in good humor, I hope. But who can live without errands and business and shopping—the nitty-gritty of surviving? Anyway, I suppose I learn from every delay, every interruption, every problem—solved or not.

There, I've *almost* talked myself into being willing to skip work on the novel today....

January 15
St. Augustine

Back once more in my favorite room at the Marion Motor Lodge in St. Augustine, waiting for Dena, after two good days alone during which I feel I have at long last managed a comprehensive grasp of the period to be encompassed by my story. I know the sequence of events—political and family—well enough to be able to fill in at least most of the gaps in my chronology once Dena arrives with her new information. What would I do on this novel, in particular, without her? I might just as well put it down in words: The story of Margaret Seton Fleming and Hibernia, I now realize, *is the most difficult to date.* The cast of characters is so vast and their interconnection so complex that it is a challenge not only to sort them out but to keep the story line simple enough so that neither the reader nor the author becomes bogged down.

I also realize that once I'm writing steadily on the novel itself, making entries in this diary can become burdensome as well as helpful. (It is helpful to me emotionally, I think.) I've never tried to write two books at once before. I can't imagine what entanglements may lie ahead. Especially when both are to be finished in the time I would normally take for one. Research, in spite of the help I've had, has already required two months longer than for any of my other five novels.

Dena and I will visit Mrs. Dorothy Austin in Hibernia day after tomorrow. This allows us a full day and a half for study and discussion together first. Good.

January 18

Dena has come and gone. Our time with Dorothy Austin was both helpful and pleasurable. She is a pretty, gentle, warm-hearted lady—with delicious humor and so much love. I knew

55

she was pleased to have me doing the story of her family and grandmother, but I felt an unexpected rapport with her— heart to heart. She had just finished reading *The Beloved Invader*. Our faiths match. This, I feel, we both know without words. Jane, her daughter, was there. About fifteen minutes into our conversation, my head went (wham!), but I don't think even Dena knew. I'm sick mentioning it.

Not only did I learn much needed information about Dorothy Austin's handsome father, Frederic (Margaret's strong, reliable son), I stood for a long time studying a large picture of him that hangs over Dorothy's bed. I wonder if the members of these families have any idea how much I learn from such seemingly casual encounters. One interesting moment during the visit: I was telling Jane and Dorothy *my* concept of one of Margaret's seven children—Belle. I had learned from Hester Williams that she (Belle) was "a little fey." But beyond that, I had come up with these characteristics: Belle was self-centered, stubborn, lazy (got out of work when possible) and felt the world owed her a living. Also, she was the one child who had more or less pooh-poohed her mother Margaret's teaching that we all do have the *obligation to hope*. In the novel, Margaret will preface that teaching with the necessity for responsible living. This, Belle would hate. (My reason for "needing" Belle to be like this has to do with the ending I planned for the entire novel.)

As I spoke of my concept of Belle, I couldn't miss the look of amazement on Dorothy Austin's face. When I finished, she said: "You must have known her! The only thing you missed about Aunt Belle was her fiery red hair!"

January 22
Back on St. Simons

I stayed one more day alone in St. Augustine, leaving my room only for some exercise and meals. Today, with the new onslaught of mail—the kind which cannot be delayed, and still more government forms to send to Beth Edwards— I am holding my breath for fear I'll lose my firm grasp of the entire story. But I intend to work at my desk today for as long as I have to in order to dive into the chronology again tomorrow with my newfound facts.

January 25

Three long days of writing by hand on a huge white tablet, and the chronology of Margaret Fleming's life *is down*. No one could decipher it but me, which is all right, since I'm the one who will have to read it through the year. My longtime friend, Easter Straker, of Lima, Ohio, gave me this magnificently large tablet years ago. It has reposed on a shelf in an office cupboard until suddenly I remembered how perfectly it would suit my need for the vast amount of space the chronology of this long novel requires. With all this space, I can still scribble in the new material one inevitably comes by as the writing goes along. For the past three days I have dived back and forth across my office in and out of one and then another research folder—going smoothly for an hour, then wasting an hour hunting for something I'd refiled for "better access" and lost. But, the chronology is finally down and, now, I will spend whatever time is required to transcribe this diary from my scrawl into type, and clear my desk. Then, at long last. I'll begin again with the novel itself.

Last night, Frances Pitts and Elsie came for dinner and I told them the entire story from memory. They were entranced and it helped me enormously. (Although I take their affection for me into consideration here!) Once these pages are up to date, I'll be back with Margaret. Actually at work, after the long research, on her story.

January 28

With this entry, the diary is current and for the remainder of this day (three or four working hours left)—I will answer mail. No good attempting to begin a novel after so much typing and so many calls handled.

Since I last wrote in these pages, I received two letters of note to me: One from Edmund Fuller, warm and buoyant, and the second from Margaret Seton Fleming's great-granddaughter Jane Rowley, at Hibernia.

Jane's letter is of particular interest here. During my recent visit to Hibernia, Jane and her mother had told me about Mrs. Phoebe Frazier of Chicago, who had attended the one hundredth anniversary service at Margaret's little church. Phoebe Frazier had gone in memory of her grandmother, whom we already knew as Maum Betty, a faithful Fleming servant and friend. The anniversary service, by the way, was observed on or near April 6, 1978, because Margaret Fleming was buried from the half-finished church on April 6, 1878. Her service was the first ever held there. In the body of Jane's letter to me, she copied a portion of a letter she had just received from Phoebe Frazier, who had sent a generous contribution to the church "for my grandmother." Maum Betty and her husband, July, were the only Fleming servants about whom we knew anything. Having tried and failed to find a listing in Chicago for Phoebe Frazier, I have written to her, asking for a number and a convenient time when I might call for a good talk. Dena had learned already that many of the antebellum servants at Hibernia were free Negroes. I know also from Ms. Frazier's letter that Margaret's son Frederic, who was master of Hibernia at the time, conducted the burial service for Maum Betty in 1911 and that he was obviously devoted to her. By the way, the word *Maum* is a phonetic spelling of the way coastal Negroes pronounced the name which denotes deep respect. Some writers use *Mammy*, others *Ma'm*. I decided to stay consistent with *Maum*, since I'd used that spelling throughout the other novels.

January 30
I lost yesterday where writing is concerned, except for some long-distance calls for further missing information to add to my totally unwieldy stack of research material. The day was unexpectedly devoted (without devotion!) to business. An IRS mix-up with one of my publishers had to be untangled. If I'd made as much as the publishing house slip said I'd made, I'd never be able to pay my tax. It is all clear now and no one's to blame but the computer. There was other business to handle too, not interesting enough to record. But today is another matter: The first

eight pages of the Prologue are rewritten from the rough, rough version done before Christmas with my head spinning.

It may still turn out to be a part of Chapter 1, but my inclination is to make these eight pages a Prologue. My late editor Tay Hohoff hated prologues, but did agree that now and then one is indicated. Somehow, although I can't ask her, I feel she'd agree that this is one of those "now and then" times. The scene is the funeral service, on a cold winter day, of Augustina Cortez Fleming, Lewis Fleming's first wife, who died after only ten years of marriage. The friendship between Margaret and Louisa Fatio has been established *and* at this unlikely moment Margaret's realization that she loves Lewis and can wait for him.

Frances Pitts came to dinner last night. I read the opening scene aloud. Results? More than encouraging from both Joyce and Frances. I value their critical opinions. They love me enough to be honest. Frances will go with us and Elsie Goodwillie to Hibernia on February 7. I'm looking forward to Frances's face when first we drive off busy Route 17 back down, with breathtaking swiftness, the shady lane into the nineteenth century. Although the big house at Hibernia is gone, the trees, the streaks of light and shadow, the river, and the cemetery beside Margaret's little church are there as they were. Tourists who zip down interstates through north Florida without exploration are missing beauty. It takes some searching, but much primitive beauty remains. It requires little imagination to "see" Hibernia plantation as it was. No imagination at all to understand why people from the North favored the spot as they surely did, especially during Margaret's later years. But, I'm racing ahead and must stop and roll in page 9.

I've made my regular Wednesday morning call to Mother and Nancy. When they are fine, as today, I am freed in my mind to work. Late start, but the kind of Island day in which I love to write: For a few minutes, gray, overcast skies, enough wind to keep the branches of the tall oaks and pines nodding encouragement; then, as I've written in perhaps more than one novel, "a lamp is turned up" and the sun picks out and illuminates even the gnarled branches of the big oak that stands deepest in our woods. A writing day. No one coming. No repairmen in the offing. No errands. Not even one guilty tremor when I glance at the growing stack of unanswered letters.

A writing day. We shall see.

February 3

A sunny Saturday on St. Simons and I have that sense of being at "home" again in what I believe May Sarton calls "the real world": I'm actually at work, oh joy, *writing* another novel. Main research finished. It seems such a long, long time since I've known this good, inner continuity. I've traveled and autographed and done TV shows and written two nonfiction books since I did *Maria*. My " native air" is to sit at this desk and see the threads— historical and genealogical—of a novel come together. I'm smiling. That sounds as though I merely sit here and watch it happen—entranced. For the past few days, during which I decided that the first eight pages are, indeed, a Prologue—and yesterday and the day before as Chapter 1 stacked up beside my typewriter, slow page after slow page—my back has ached, my shoulders, my head, all because I'm writing again. Joy? You bet. The aches and pains are part of it. Tension, obviously, from sitting so long, from the mere physical act of so much typing after the months of research—and from the glorious discontent of *having* to do it. Discontent? I don't believe anyone writes without it. Or paints. Or composes music.

I look about at my friends who are genuinely content without the inner drive I never cease to feel. I will never know contentment and would loathe it. I'm sure. Be bored with it would feel utterly strange with the feeling. A kind gentleman made for me a handsome brown and beige needlepoint copy of a poem by Mary Brent Whiteside. I don't know this man. He did all that loving work as a thank you for some small thing, but whether or not he realized it, he chose the most apt poem. A few lines course steadily through my mind these days. Lines from the beginning and end of the poem:

Who has known heights and depths shall not again
Know peace
. . . .
Who once has trodden stars seeks peace no more.

I would use the word *contentment* instead of *peace*. The peace
of God can hold steadfastly in the human heart through anything. But I'm sure the poet used the word *peace* as I use the word
contentment. Lack of a goad toward those "stars." The trodding
of stars to me, at least, involves pain, tears, the will to push, to
refuse a reprieve. I will die, or at least I will want to die, when I
can no longer feel the goad, the glorious, gladsome, galling goad
of another gigantic job to do.

Chapter 1, finished late yesterday, may not read like it, but
for me, it was a day of exhilaration. It is a quiet chapter and one
I didn't mean to write at all when I sat down here two mornings
ago. But there it is now in front of me on the corner of my desk.
A small stack of yellow paper. Understand, I do not praise my
writing when I say things of this kind, but with evidence of any
measure of talent (all God-given, whether the writer knows it
or not) comes mystery. Where does a book come from? Oh, of
course, Dena and Hester and my other loyal friends have helped
me assemble a staggering amount of excellent research material.
And yet, here is Chapter 1, breathing, I think, of its own accord.
Margaret's husband, Lewis Fleming, and his two sons by his first
wife are *people* now. I know the sound of their voices, the color
of their hair and eyes; and so swiftly that the days are not long
enough to keep up, I am learning about their personality quirks
and weaknesses and strengths. Frances Pitts, after reading what
is now the Prologue, said, "Margaret and Louisa Fatio are right
there—living." I hope Frances is right. But, where did they come
from?

The author knows least of all.

Today, another late start. An hour on long-distance—a happy hour—with Mother and Nancy (they were snow-bound up

north), a letter I just had to write, my daily call to Ruby Wilson, who, at home, has adjusted so remarkably to the loss of her leg that I think I call her for *my* sake, not hers. And now these lines written here. This afternoon. Chapter 2.

Joyce and I have been on the Scarsdale Medical Diet for nearly two weeks. It works and it isn't at all boring. Today, lunch is an enormous fresh fruit salad—one of my favorite meals on the menu. Joyce is downstairs in the kitchen peeling and slicing. I will love every bite of the salad, every word of conversation with Joyce, but restlessness will plague me until I'm back here beginning Chapter 2.

Even then it will go on. I hope—forever. This kind of discontent—not dissatisfaction—discontent—is my native air. I marvel at the mystery that comes with the start of each new novel.

With me, at least, this is not true of nonfiction books.

That's a mystery, too.

February 6

The Prologue, Chapters 1 and 2 are down. A good start. Tomorrow, Joyce, Elsie, Frances and I leave for St. Augustine for "geography research." Why does the mere writing of that line elevate me? Love for the old city and the history of its surrounding area, yes. But also the minute I walk into my little motel room, I seem inevitably to realize all over again that I'm actually away and embarked on further adventure. Crazy? Of course. There will be an accumulation of mail when I return and the telephone will ring again. But I will be refreshed. This trip is partly a birthday celebration for dear Elsie and to give loyal, involved Frances a real-life look at Margaret's little church at Hibernia and to let me look at the land, the roads and the river.

I also need to tie up some loose ends on research, and one of the good hours of the time will be the one spent at Hibernia with Margaret's granddaughter, my new friend Dorothy Austin, in her lovely living room overlooking the vast St. Johns.

And, I will go with a singularly light heart: My head seems better and the mail is no longer stacked on my desk unanswered. Yesterday, I either wrote, dictated or notated for Lorrie Carlson, my longtime friend and helper, some seventy letters. There are no words to communicate my relief. What would I do without her?

Today, I pay bills and get my hair cut and sign books in three Island shops. "Too bad it's such a rainy day," a friend said on the telephone this morning. I couldn't care less. I love the Island in the rain, the mail is caught up and I'm going to north Florida! For three whole days.

February 14

I love Valentine's Day. Real or only half real, the heart is uppermost for at least one day.

Joyce, Frances Pitts, Elsie, and I returned late on February 10 from a productive and fun time in St. Augustine. Mostly, in fact, *around* St. Augustine. Our first stop, dictated by my heart, was at Dorothy Austin's house at Hibernia. Her quiet, thoughtful son, Larry Austin, whom I met that day for the first time, designed his mother's house so that she can lie in her bed and look right out at the St. Johns River—two miles across toward the deep woods at New Switzerland where her antecedents, the prominent and fascinating Fatio family, once lived. We drove and Larry Austin took his mother to Margaret's church in a golf cart. Jane Rowley, his sister, after several rather futile but sincere efforts to reach some of the black people in the neighborhood for me, went along and for more than an hour, I let the tiny, clapboard English country church become the center of my very being. I truly have never seen more beautiful coloring in stained-glass windows. The window in memory of Margaret, high over the tiny altar, is breathtaking on a sunny day—as was that day. In the center is a ruby red cross—just right for Margaret, as I am coming to know her. The blues are myriad and oh, so subtle.

We lingered still longer in the little cemetery behind the church where lie the earthly remains of many of my characters. Frances Pitts stood as she always stands in the presence of great, ancient trees, hands clasped, in silence. Finally, as we walked together back to the car, she whispered to me: "Genie, standing there by the grave of Augustina, Lewis Fleming's first wife, I— became Margaret!" This is not as far out as it sounds. Frances has that capacity. She also knew my Prologue—the actual burial of the much loved young Augustina Cortez Fleming— the scene bearing, I hope, the seeds of the entire novel. I knew Frances was able to view that very scene from Margaret's viewpoint. Margaret Seton, at age nineteen. My response may have sounded flip. Frances didn't think so. She knows me too well. "If you did become Margaret, for heaven's sake, tell me what she's thinking."

These days—these days passing right now, excluding that brief time down there in Margaret's land—are, it seems, more tense and chaotic for me *inside* than during any novel I've tried yet. Any little hint from anyone helps.

I'm scared. But being scared is nothing new at this stage. The difference between the extent of the fright at the start of this novel and the others is that this fear lasts longer. *Maria's* story line was straight and clear. *Don Juan's* not so clear and, next to this one, I despaired more over *Don Juan McQueen* than any other. The anxious times over Margaret Fleming's story (wish I had a title!) simply go on longer. Will I *ever* get it all down? Nearly fifty years of a life lived through two wars. I have, of course, come to expect the anxiety I feel today—the straining at the bit all day Sunday, trying to rest; all day Monday of this week while going from dentist's office to the eye doctor; and, yesterday, when the accumulated mail kept me away from this diary and the novel— all add to the jitters.

Last night a happy dinner with Sarah Plemmons and Pat Lynch, from Connecticut, and I did enjoy every minute. After all, we ate at my friend Alfonza Ramsey's Plantation Club and he serves the best steaks anywhere. But always, clamoring within me, Margaret, Lewis, their children, the tangle of two wars, the necessity of learning the social customs and mores of Margaret's day— and how to pare down the cast, yes, there were so many. I'll have to eliminate whole branches of both the Fatio and Fleming families.

The trip to north Florida was a productive geography lesson for me. Joyce, who can find any obscure place and still drive like a pro, helped locate old Fort Heilman—one of the primitive beauty spots just outside the town of Middleburg. We sat for a long time also beside the St. Johns at Tocoi, at the point we are certain the little steamer from Hibernia landed—not only with tourists from the North, but often with Margaret and some of her children en route to visit with Louisa Fatio in St. Augustine. From the Tocoi landing, a horse-drawn train rolled some sixteen miles east through wilderness (now cleared for farming) to the San Sebastian River at the edge of the old town of St. Augustine. If the tide was right, travelers could then take the ferry across that river and on the other side be picked up by carriages and driven to their destinations in the city.

Our route followed the old horse-drawn railroad-track bed.

So, a few more hazy spots have been cleared for me. Everyone is pulling for me who knows about the fact that I'm attempting two books at once. Elsie Goodwillie, who has typed with such love and patience and care and skill through every manuscript I've done since 1964, seems more involved with Margaret's story than any to date. And yesterday's mail brought a letter from my friend by correspondence in Philadelphia, the author and playwright Constance O'Hara, which helped my sagging confidence more than she will ever know. Sternly, she admonished me that I must stop considering myself "just a popular writer." True, I do consciously write in what I hope will be a widely understood style. I don't try for great art. I don't believe I possess that much talent. But I need to reread a portion of her letter today. This is some of what Constance wrote; "Genie, stop it! You are a writer of quality. I don't know any better writing than your treatment of Shays' Rebellion in Lighthouse. The landscape of the south, because of your writing of it, is before me. The opening of New Moon Rising simply is the experience of a packet on the Inland Waterways to St. Simons. Like Horace Gould, your reader feels the darkness and the sense of unfallen rain—the damp, intense heat. Lady writers of historical novels do get the silent treatment in the New York Review of Books. (The lady writers are, in the main, a reasonably sickening lot!) You are not one of them—you are a widely recognized novelist—no more uneven than Dickens—and growing from book to book." (That helps most of all!)

Now to sit and think for whatever time is required until I find out—from somewhere inside or outside my own head—what is wrong with my first two rough chapters. The facts are there, but Joyce and Frances and I all agree (no one else has read them) that there is too much talk, not enough action. They need to be restructured. Perhaps by using Margaret in one of them? Who knows? Maybe all I have needed is uninterrupted time. Maybe my fears and confusions are groundless.

Oh well, a year from now I'll know all that happened with the story of Margaret Seton Fleming and her beautiful Hibernia.

February 15, 1979

As always, it seems that other, unrelated, matters keep me from writing first thing in the morning. Today, though, part of the delay at least, was fun. Bob Smith, owner of The Booksmith in St. Augustine, appeared on Virginia Atter Keyes's radio talk show from Jacksonville. Joyce finally found it on the dial and I couldn't resist calling both Virginia, whom we like so much, and Bob. He did a marvelous job and the entire show was stimulating. We really care about Bob and Diana Smith. They're genuine book lovers and Bob writes superior reviews. One good thing to antic-ipate—Diana is coming to the Island to consult with our friend Dr. Dietrich, who examined me the first time I had vertigo. (My head is mostly good these days. Almost always dizzy first thing in the morning but it does wear off, and only now and then returns during the day or evening, if I bend a certain way—such as in laying the fire, or closing shutters.) Diana Smith will spend next Wednesday night with us. Good.

No matter how minor the interruptions, by the time I get to work I am uptight and will be until I get these first two chap-ters to suit me. Worked hard on Chapter 1 yesterday. Improved. But last night as we watched *Julius Caesar* on Public Television, a whole new idea struck me. Afraid even Shakespeare can't keep my mind off Margaret Fleming.

Another delay today: Had to write a biography of myself for use at a Humanities meeting where I will appear at the University of Charleston in my hometown late next month. I continue to believe myself when I say I'll take no more dates, so never have a prepared biography, and this time I sent one of the two remaining publicity pictures. This date was made long ago though. And it will delight Mother and give us our visit in the spring instead of June, as always. And— I will then, please God, have the entire summer to work.

February 17

Two long days of very hard work. The Prologue stands, at least, for now. Chapters 1 and 2 completely reworked, added to, so that they are now three chapters. Good enough until rewrite time. Manuscript page 46. Fifteen pages today in spite of an hour's call to Mother and Nance. It is Saturday afternoon. Late. I'm supposed to rest every day—doctor's orders—thank goodness. It's my best reading time. Still reveling in the masterful piece of work Arthur Schlesinger did on *Robert Kennedy and His Times*. No work tomorrow, Sunday. I am jealous of our Sundays alone here in the woods. I like this coastal winter weather. Cool fifties, windy, gray, the trees in constant motion.

The mail is stacking up again. I ignore it.

February 19, 1979

It was nearly noon when I returned from a dental appointment yesterday. As usual, I was frustrated. But, when I walked in the house, Joyce had read the entire three chapters and had written a note which said in part: "This all seems to evolve so easily and at a natural tempo. . . . You've covered a load of history, but not at the expense of the characters. These people are obviously already so familiar to you! I'm eager to know how they will interact." Her opinion, if it's positive, has never, in all the years, failed to give me confidence. Joyce feels that, so far in the rough draft, I am a touch shy on description, but all that can come in the final rewrite. The note was signed: "With pride. Your Pard." She is my "pardner" and, close as we are, I wonder at times if she really believes how deeply I value her thinking.

Today could be—should be—a good workday. No one is coming and I am getting an early start. Much of the northeast coast is choked with snow and ice. The Island sky is bright-dark: clear sunshine and then winter gray, with wind. I just looked for a long moment out over the back marsh—small, compared to the vast one that stretches away from the other side of our house across to Brunswick on the mainland. A look out my bedroom window always brings to mind the Eddie Thompsons, our neighbors, whose home is barely visible through the trees. Today, I breathed a prayer for Frieda Thompson because Eddie died last week suddenly. How different the beauty around their house must appear to her now.

Yesterday, after lunch, I made a feeble, exploratory start on Chapter 4. Not successful. Except in forcing me to realize that now is the time to face untangling Lewis Fleming's part in the Second Seminole War. Dena has me well stocked with research material. In no time, I stopped trying to write and picked up a little-known out-of-print book titled *Reminiscences of The Second Seminole War* by John Bemrose. Bemrose was a very young Englishman, a mercenary in the United States Army in the year which concerns me now—1836. He has written an enormously valuable book. In surprisingly readable language, he describes the Battle of Withlacoochee in which Lewis Fleming was severely wounded. All needed details are here—far more than I need. Selecting only pertinent facts makes for one of my big problems. How to tie in all that was happening to the family at the same time? Their house was burned by Indians. How to blend the two sudden bursts of action—fire and war—into a smooth narrative? Do I handle the battle in the scene with Lewis and Bemrose, the medical assistant who cared for him? Do I handle some of it inside Margaret's head as she is caring for Lewis's children? And what device will I use to bridge the time from 1833 in Chapter 3 to 1835 just before Christmas in Chapter 4? One thing sure. I won't find out by examining my confusion.

Half of the Bemrose book is read. Perhaps covering the last half will give me a clue for the actual writing.

February 20
Yesterday, I bought a new typewriter and a new copying ma-

chine. Both needed. My old Olympia (manual) was rattling like a gun carriage over a corduroy road during the Seminole War. Mr. Davidson, from whom we buy all our office supplies, made three trips to the house yesterday so as not to disturb our work today. Such a kind and gracious gentleman. Our old copier, which required all sorts of messy liquids, had completely stopped functioning just when Joyce really needed it for her current manuscript: *A Book of Praises.*

I'm stalling, putting off the hard decisions re the Seminoles. Enough.

February 21

Late start at my desk. Exterminator, electrician and insurance agent measuring house for some vague reason. Also, another quick trip to the dentist today. Diana Smith, co-owner of The Booksmith in St. Augustine, drove to the Island today to see Dr. Dietrich and us. She began the Scarsdale Medical Diet with us at lunch. Tonight, I will charcoal-broil lamb chops and Joyce will make a salad. I've lost nearly thirteen pounds. I enjoy Diana so much, it required real discipline for me to wave her off with Joyce to see the churchyard and Island. But I got out of focus yesterday on the novel. I moved too directly to characterization when what was needed, I now see, was exposition explaining the Second Seminole War. *And,* just when I had lost Pat Wickman's telephone number and needed the material she was researching for me at The P. K. Yonge Library in Gainesville, Monroe Wilson, our right-hand man, brought in the mail and there was Pat's material. On cue.

Pat Wickman, one of my favorite people on earth, is in school at Gainesville, Florida, these days. She has helped me unstintingly with research on two novels—now three. Any trip to St. Augustine for the past five years has meant much time spent by choice with Pat. I miss her more than she suspects.

I'll do very well to get down my notes on the Indian trouble preparatory to rewriting Chapter 4 tomorrow. A long-distance call to Dena just clarified one or two important points. And, as usual, with Dena, I had good laughs.

Diana will spend the night. Should be a beautiful, relaxing evening. That is, if I am ever truly relaxed about anything at this early stage of a big novel.

February 23

Not much page progress but lots of clarification on the tangle of Fleming-Fatio families and the start of the Second Seminole War. A hard day of mostly study and seven acceptable pages for the slowly mounting stack of rough draft. Another fortuitous happening for me: In yesterday's mail, just minutes after I'd asked Joyce when she thought steamboats began to be used on the St. Johns River, came a surprise envelope from Jackie Bearden at the St. Augustine Historical Society Library. A clearly written article on the very subject and I hadn't even asked for it. Now, I know. There were actually steamboats there as early as 1834 and 1835. I may have to rewrite a page or two from yesterday's work, but no matter. I'm delighted. And just called Jackie to tell her that her ESP is working. Also—"God's in His heaven" and all's right with my funny world as I manage to go on straddling two centuries. My head was woozy when I woke up today, but I got up too fast in order to hear the latest news on China's invasion of Vietnam after Vietnam's invasion of Cambodia. I am head-deep in the Second Seminole War—primitive transportation, primitive medical attention, which now seems only brutal, battles fought over unmapped terrain—but one word current then is still current—*war*.

February 24

It is Saturday, but I'm working as usual. Yesterday, I finished a new Chapter 4. Today, in checking some material, I see I need to change only a few things—all minor. I understand better now how some of the Fleming and Fatio Negroes came to be "Free Persons of Color." Some had rendered special service and so were freed as a reward, but in the main they were free because they had, during the second Spanish period (1783-1821), run away from Georgia or South Carolina owners and found protection with the Spanish. Accustomed to their homes and work, most stayed on after the Americans took over. They received no pay and, depending upon the character of the owner, were treated much the same as slaves. Even a "Free Person of Color" needed a sponsor. In my story, I will decide, since there are no records, whether or not Maum Easter, Maum Betty, their husbands Pompey and July, were free or slave.

My Saturday telephone conversation with Mother and Nance was good. They are fine and their snow was melted by an almost springlike rain. I leave March 20 to spend two weeks with them. While there I will keep the commitment at the University of Charleston. Joyce will join me at Mother's on April 1. On April 3, we fly to New York on publishing business and on April 9 to Grand Rapids, where we appear at a Zondervan sales conference and have some fun with Carol Holquist and our editor, Judy Markham.

I had trouble getting to sleep last night—rare for me. And, of course, I thought about the novel. It came strongly that I need to spend more time in study of St. Augustine as it was in the years in which I'm currently working—the 1830s. I have learned that almost half of the city's population was black or mulatto. Many of them Free Negroes—yet, not really free. They lived with all sorts of restrictions. One example—no "person of color" could give a party in his own house without permission of the mayor!

The excellent material Dena sent on plantation life—actually a diary by a gentleman planter, a Fleming neighbor named Reed, will tell me exactly which vegetables froze in Lewis's Hibernia garden the night of the devastating freeze of 1835 in which he lost all his orange trees. The freeze occurred in February—by then, he would have planted English peas, artichokes, celery, potatoes, beets, carrots, etc. I will add this to Chapter 4 when I make the Free Negro changes.

It is nearly noon. I have interrupted hard study of facts and dates to make this entry. Even if I work late, I may not get to any further writing—which will take Lewis into the Second Seminole War and bring devastation to his family and to his first cousins, Louisa and Sophia Fatio, across the St. Johns River at New Switzerland.

I will need some thinking time before writing. Still wondering—will I handle the Seminole action at the scene with Lewis? Nothing may turn out as I think today. But, there will come a time when the current of the novel itself will begin to carry me along. A novelist who writes pure fiction must wing. I am, of course, always having to stop and study or look up something. I have no strong desire to drop the writing of historical fiction. I am hooked on coastal history. Especially Florida history. What I would love is history as a background, but fictionized characters. A letter yesterday from a lady in Richmond, Virginia, really gave me a lift. I had written to tell her that I was working on a novel set in Florida during the Civil War. She was lyrical.

February 26

Joyce and I have just stopped for lunch. Today, cold sliced steak from last night's celebration. Steak night on the menu is, along with lamb chop night, not only my favorite but my night to shine. I charcoal-broil steaks and chops, and that, let it here be recorded, is the only kind of cooking which I like. Preparing the fuel for an evenly burning bed of coals is an exacting art and I enjoy it.

Yesterday, Sunday, was a fun day—we read by a small fire which we really didn't need. It was raining and degrees outside. After one blaze-up, we let the fire die. Today, I am grateful for yesterday's quiet. Since early morning, I have been in trauma. I expected it. I got up at seven—ready. Even eager. I have lost count of the hours spent in hard study, digesting the complex and totally primitive military operations leading up to the Battle of Withlacoochee at the start of the Second Seminole War. But with the weekend study of the late Rembert Patrick's excellent book on General Duncan L. Clinch—sent by Dena in the nick of time—I felt the moment had come for me to dive into what may turn out to be one of the really difficult parts of the entire novel. I girded myself and was hard at work by 9 A.M., following more study. And when Joyce called me to eat at noon, I was literally shaking. My head ached, my back ached and my brain sizzled.

But, as soon as I finish this entry. I'm ready for Lewis Fleming to leave his family and go into war as a brigade inspector (rank of major) in the volunteer Florida Horse Regiment.

I wrote hard (there is no other word) for nearly two hours and then discovered I had skipped a part of a year and had to rewrite! But, nothing was wasted. When God is involved, I cling to my long-held belief that with Him nothing *needs* to be wasted. More verification—had I not written those pages in the wrong sequence, I might have missed the perspective I needed. Writing time on any novel is the best of times for me, never mind the aches and pains and shakes, but a touch of envy creeps in when I am handling a battle or a treaty—envy of those who can simply sit down with completed research and write it out for a nonfiction book or article. I must figure it out, of course, but running on several tracks—I have the added burden (and excitement!) of staying alert for description, characterization, reader response, emotional buildup, and so on.

We heard the noon news. It was mainly battle reports as the Chinese invade Vietnam. At lunch break, too, I learned that Sarah Edmond's daughter had been slashed across the hand at school by a fellow student who was evidently attempting to "prove" his manhood. Sarah, who is shining up our house today, is a contained, poised, fearless lady. Most mothers would be basket cases had that just occurred to their child.

Strange, perplexing parallels crowd my thoughts: Horror at the primitive encounters that shattered the lives of people who lived in the last century in north Florida—just down the coast from where I write. The Seminole wars, when both Indians and white settlers killed, scalped, even disemboweled each other. Chinese and Vietnamese, with modern, so-called sophisticated weapons, rain death and destruction on homes and factories. And, as in the year 1835, " settlers," who, after all, are just people living in houses on land—stream down roads seeking safety from the destruction just as "settlers" streamed to safety back then into the makeshift military fortifications made of logs and wooden pickets. One woman, whose husband was murdered in 1835, was herself scalped—and lived.

I'm too deep in the preparation for the Battle of Withla-coochee to draw any profound observations about unchanging human nature. I doubt that there are any to be drawn. But I know I'd be in a far deeper nervous turmoil at this moment had the cedar waxwings not distracted me happily as I worked at the business of finding the right way to enter Lewis's battle. All morning, they have (fighting a stiff northwest wind) attacked the holly tree outside my office window—intent upon gobbling the last winter berry. From the corner of my eye, when I began work, I could see red holly berries. Now—green holly branches. We planted all our berry trees for the birds, though. As I moved detachments of soldiers and fortified plantations, I cheered on the waxwings—and took moments of relief to laugh at our neurotic mockingbird, who goes quite berserk at the appearance of even one stray waxwing.

Next chapter. Lewis Fleming is about to get his orders to leave his three children in the care of Maum Easter and the other Hibernia servants and go off to that battle.

March 1

A perfect Island spring day. Chapter 6 is finished and also Chapter 7. Both in rough, of course and may not turn out to be 6 and 7 in the final draft. But quite simply, I can suddenly write here that I haven't been so happy or felt so well (head good this morning—no medication!) in months. I actually feel like myself today. Not pressured—even with so much business travel up ahead—just happy. Problems abound, but they are suddenly no bigger than I! Of course, much of my joy springs from the fact that I feel like me again, but even that is undoubtedly due to my being once more—finally, after two non-fiction books—back in my real world of another novel. Sometimes I feel like a simpleton. I am so simple and obvious to me right now. In separate ways, I enjoyed writing both *St. Simons Memoir* and *Leave Yourself Alone*. Neither were novels, though, and therein lies the clue to my funny mind.

Some of my happy feeling today is due to a marvelously foolish, and, to one so work-bound as I, daring thing Joyce and I have on the spur of the moment decided to do. President and Mrs. Carter have invited us to the White House on March 1 for—of all marvelous things—an Andrés Segovia classical guitar concert. My first reaction was—*now*? On this tight work schedule? True, we may never get another such invitation, but why not next year when the pressure of work is off? "I wish we could," I said to Joyce. "I just can't spare the time. Especially since I'll be away for nearly a month only a week later."

Suddenly, I thought—why not? Of course, it's expensive, but when have we done anything, gone anywhere (except to visit our mothers) when one or both of us did not have to appear on TV or radio, sign books or make a speech of some kind? "Let's go," I said. Being Joyce, she agreed as quickly to my change of mind as she had to my first rejection. So, we're going. I confess I am ex- cited now at the thought of being in the same room with the president we love and believe in—*and* Andrés Segovia! A lot of people say a lot of nasty things about Jimmy Carter. One thing you have to say is that he is a man of *superior taste*. Leontyne Price, Horowitz—and now Segovia.

This may not be true when next I write here, but, for now, the novel is under my control. A difficult and confusing section to handle—I keep missing a small point or goofing up my geography—but there is always the rewrite. One never just writes a book. One rewrites it. Even in the rough draft. I like my people and my story more and more. This is a good, good day. So why not say so?

March 2

Up early to do an introduction for another author's book. A promise kept. After coffee and our diet breakfast of protein toast and grapefruit (I've now lost nearly seventeen pounds) and some political discussion following the news, I heard *him*: one bright sign of spring for which we wait from one early March to the next, the first song—silvery bars tossed on the air in regular ten-second intervals—from our newly returned painted bunting. For love of Richard Baltzell, a publishing friend, we have named the first bunting of the year Richard. I opened my door, dashed out onto the upstairs porch, listened for ten seconds to be sure, and yelled for Joyce. *He is here.* We won't actually see him for a month. He lives and eats in the tops of the tall pines for roughly five weeks. Then, one day in April, there he will be—a small creature of crimson, blue, chartreuse and rich brown, as much at home at our feeders as though he hadn't been in Central America all winter. A kind of security and sense of play invariably return with this brightly colored little bird.

Later

Long writing day. I'm quitting. Thirteen pages on the novel— well into Chapter 9. I am best when coping with multiple emotions: My reaction to these days, spring on the Island, painted bunting calls, and the hideous horror of the Seminole War!

March 5

Yesterday, Sunday, March 4, was the most memorable day we've had in a long time. Why? It marked nineteen years that Joyce and I have shared a home and the fact of our totally satisfying, lengthening " history" simply made us both happy. We stuck with the Scarsdale Diet until dinner, when—to celebrate—along with the permit- ted steak and salad, we sampled some excellent Beaujolais we'd kept for an occasion. Certainly our friendship is so solid, so mutually respectful, so time-tested, it must be fairly rare.

We read and listened to music all day.

It is after lunch on Monday as I write and our well-laid plans to go to the White House for the Segovia concert may be sky high. For one thing, my head is funny today again and *not* to go would undoubtedly be better for me, especially with the long month's travel up ahead to West Virginia, New York and Grand Rapids. Now, the news at noon, with word that, once more, the president (we were going mainly to see him) has come up with a possible breakthrough on the Middle East stalemate. He and the First Lady leave Washington on Wednesday for Egypt. Saturday in Israel. There is no way either Jimmy or Rosalyn could be there at the concert on Sunday next. But, before we decide finally, we will wait through a few more newscasts this afternoon. And then, Joyce will call the White House. At least, we're proud that we were flexible enough to decide to go in the midst of new books *and* that we're now equally flexible about canceling the trip.

I am working so intensely today on the actual scene at the Battle of Withlacooche during the Second Seminole War that I could scarcely eat my lunch.

March 8

So much is going on—friends to hospital. New York publishing engagements to make by long-distance, the president in Egypt and Israel on a courageous, singular effort to make peace. I try valiantly to keep up with the news on my little desk radio. I do care. And, along with every other American who cares and remembers Dallas and Jack Kennedy in 1963, hold my breath every time Jimmy Carter stands up in an open car in a motorcade. He is such an original thinker, few understand him, and what some can't understand, they criticize.

Things are quiet and peaceful at Mother's and this helps.

I can't quite see how I'd keep at the novel daily, as I've done, on days when my head is both good (as today) and bad (as yesterday) without Nancy to care for Mother. But I keep at it and don't forget that these days are, of all my days, the best for me. I surprise myself at being able to ignore the mounting mail stack. It must be answered sometime, but, I rationalize—not today, and today is what I have. Next week will be hospital week for us. Ruby Wilson goes back for painful treatment, our friend, Teensie Bradshaw, coeditor of *The Islander*, goes back, and now dear Jimmie Harnsberger will have major surgery in Macon. God is in charge, I remind myself and roll another canary sheet into my typewriter.

I complain at times about straddling two centuries at once. To be honest, I revel in it. One house on the St. Johns burned yesterday in my novel. I must burn the other one today. The Indians really fought back at having their land gobbled up. They have my sympathy. They gave up eventually—as I confess I have almost given up on St. Simons. Developers are gobbling up the gorgeous green spaces.

I am rambling here—probably putting off the difficult writing ahead. Daily, I make an enormous leap—into it. Tonight is Frances Pitts' birthday party at Elsie's. But now I must make that concentrated leap back to the year 1836.

March 10

For the past two days, I have written so hard that when it came time in the late afternoon for my "blood pressure nap," I tumbled into bed exhausted. Today is Saturday. My long long-distance call to Mother and Nance was a happy one and they are counting the days until my plane lands on March 20. I'm counting days, too, for their reason and my own. After checking the enormous stack of unanswered mail, my count tells me I must stop work altogether on the novel no later than Wednesday of next week—even though the juices are flowing. I have my normal conflict about wanting to go while being half afraid to leave the book. But, after Charleston, New York and Grand Rapids—such a wrenching break in the flow of the work—I've decided a short trip to the very site of Margaret Fleming's home will turn the trick for me. Joyce, Frances, Elsie and I will leave after Easter for Florida for two or three days. One short visit with Dorothy Austin, Margaret's granddaughter, will bring me back to Margaret in a rush. That and a walk through Margaret's little church and its quiet, simple cemetery. Also, Dena has arranged for us to visit Mr. Clement Slade in Jacksonville, who has slides of old Hibernia as it looked when Margaret was its mistress. I will see those on the same trip. I am almost peaceful about having to stop. As peaceful as I can ever be when a novel is in progress.

Today, had Jimmy Carter not whisked off to the Middle East, we would have arrived in Washington. How many times a day I return to the twentieth century long enough to pray for the president's safety—especially now that he is in Israel. "Blessed are the peacemakers . . . " Not in my sixty-two years have I known a president to try so patiently and with such courage and persistence—for peace. He is "blessed."

I am mainly Actionizing now—Chapters 13, 14 and 15. Based, of course, on all known facts, but writing always goes more easily when I can let my imagination out, I'm through with the Second Seminole War—almost. The novel is already long. But then, my rough drafts always are. *Don Juan McQueen*'s rough ended up on page 750! In the rewrite, I pulled it down to something near 600 pages. "Hibernia" (still only my working title) covers a much longer period of time. I do wish I had the real title.

It is a glorious Island day—72 degrees and sunny. Our pear trees are bursting into bloom and yesterday, before she went to the hospital to visit Ruby, Joyce had to run from honey and bumble bees as she cut sprays of japonica to take with her. Spring has been creeping in since mid-February. It seems only yesterday that one tall gum tree I watch from my office was still hung with red autumn leaves. Gum trees need very short rest periods. Sweet gum, especially. They still have colored leaves at Christmas and by late January, their buds begin to swell.

In spite of the strenuous week's work, I, too, am bursting with life. When my funny vertigo head is good—as of this hour—I can't recall a time when I've felt better. About a lot of things.

March 12

Monday morning. Yesterday, a good and fun day of rest, just the two of us. Our weather is heady. The light has been changing from winter gold to spring green-white for days now and, today, it is very evident. Our mocking-bird, Snoopy, is everywhere, but keeping to his normal eccentric patterns, has, unlike every other mocker on the Island, sung only one day. He will sing when the others stop!

Along with the joys of a spring day and good work to do, there is anxiety, concern, irritation and disgust with some of the officials in the Middle East who seem more like prima donnas than statesmen. President Carter's voice sounded so tired when we got the radio news at eight this morning, it drained me until I brought myself up short with the reality that today I am to work on Chapter 14 of the novel and cannot carry his burdens too. We watched the Segovia concert on Public Television yesterday—the magnificent experience we could have shared. I had a few pangs. It was magnificent and I did want to be sitting there in the East Room. What is real and good and implicit with grandeur about America, I love as much as anyone.

This is hospital week for our three friends. Dear Jimmie Harnsberger is in surgery now in Macon, Georgia. We have prayed for her with so much love. Another sorrow: Curtis Stevens is dead. We bought our land from his hand- some brother, Ben, gone too. Curtis and Ben had special meaning for us. They were gentlemen of the old school. Curtis drilled our well and came to repair it the last time when he was so ill he could hardly walk. He was truly involved in what I try to do in my books laid in the coastal south. A man of keen intelligence and perception, he loved his land with an abiding reverence and pride and had a traditional Georgian's regard for history. We will miss him deeply. It will seem strange not to see to it that Curtis gets his usual copies of these two new books—this diary and the new novel about Margaret Fleming.

Another week begins—with concern about hostilities in the Middle East, and for Mary Stevens and her children and Ann Stevens Parker, Curtis's sister, our neighbor. Some butterflies for our friends in the hospital—and, yet, I have the ongoing "other world" in which I so happily live during the months of writing. I wrote all day Saturday. I've been "away" from Margaret and Lewis and Louisa Fatio and their families for only one day. I miss them. It is time to pick up the threads and begin Chapter 14.

March 13

Curtis Stevens's graveside service was held in Christ Churchyard at 2 P.M. In view of that, I decided to tackle mail today and not write on the novel. His widow, Mary, was magnificent, as were his children. And during the brief time spent beside his open grave, surrounded by flowers because everyone loved and respected him, I thought of what Curtis had taught me about his first ancestor on St. Simons, Captain Charles Stevens, who gave the very ground in which Curtis and Ben are buried to Christ Church so long ago.

All morning and for the remainder of the afternoon, I did mail, mail, mail. I miss the novel. Its people are so real to me, that I wonder about them, what they're doing and thinking when, for any reason, the process is stopped. But I did finish Chapter 14 yesterday. There is a flaw in certain earlier chapters: The action slows be- cause in my concentrated effort to get facts down, I went overboard and stayed too long in a scene with Lewis Fleming and his two sons. I see that now. It can be remedied, but I don't yet know exactly how.

March 14

Two big things, for me at least: (1) Suddenly events turned around in the Middle East. The president is still over there exerting every effort, every ounce of energy to bring about an Egyptian-Israeli peace agreement—and it seems now to be working! This, of course, is only the beginning. Israel and Egypt have been at each other's throats since antiquity. Then, I've made the tough decision not to write any more before I have to leave unless perhaps I'm free on Saturday. The amount of unanswered mail and desk work was far more than I thought. But my head has been good for almost two full days. I'm really hopeful that it may be gone for now. The vertigo, that is. Not my head. I may need that.

March 17

Jimmy Carter pulled it off! He is home. And we are extremely proud of him. I'm still whaling away at my slowly diminishing stack of personal mail. My doctor had said that my type of vertigo comes and goes, and he was right. For almost three full days I had not a trace of it and, optimist that I am, decided it had completely quit. Not so. This morning, with all this mail still to do, it is back. Oh, me.

March 18

My last Sunday at home for nearly a month. I fly to Charleston, West Virginia, on Tuesday, for the planned two weeks with Mother and Nance and Mary Jane. Since the University of Charleston appearance—called, I think, an Appalachian Festival—is on Friday, March 23, with press and a discussion panel, and since I will be forced for the duration of the trip to imprison my normally bare feet in shoes, Nancy and I will shop on my first day there. But by Saturday, March 24, I can begin to let down. Nancy and Mother are so great. With them, I am free, free. No entertaining, no guests dropping in—I sleep, I read, I have coffee in my room alone each morning. Joyce will join me April 1, and on April 3, we will take off for New York and a week in the other world I love—the publishing world. And that includes a much anticipated weekend with Carolyn Blakemore and her sister, Barbara, at their Long Island cottage. On Monday—fly to Grand Rapids, where, if my crazy head stays in place, I will have fun and stimulating talk with Dr. Bob DeVries and others of my longtime friends at Zondervan. Rather a tight Grand Rapids schedule, though: April lo, appear and speak at sales conference, luncheon, press at two, TV at four. Sandwiched in somewhere before we catch our plane back to the Island at noon the next day will be time at Zondervan's offices and a tour of their new plant.

Later Sunday

This has been a day of catching up loose ends— putting my desk away for a month and making long-distance calls. I just spoke with Dorothy Austin, whom I called for selfish reasons. I have come to love Dorothy so much, and her belief in me as an author is so reassuring, I just had to be sure she'd still be at Hibernia when I make my way back there on April 17 and 18. Two more long-distance calls to make—one to Mrs. Phoebe Frazier in Chicago, granddaughter of Maum Betty, Margaret Fleming's friend and cook. I need to know if Maum Betty was Maum Easter's daughter and if Betty was old enough to have served Margaret herself. Then, of course, again for my own sake, I must hear Dena's voice before I leave. I am dedicating the novel to Dena, but I wish I knew a more adequate way to tell her how steadily she is with me as I work. She and Hester Williams and Dorothy Austin, Jane Rowley and another great-granddaughter, Betty Ingle, all cheer me on. I dare not fail.

The sky today is cerulean blue—not one cloud. It will be 70

degrees and I have to leave it all for the still freezing north. A Christian never need worry about external weather, though. There is a way for our inner climate to remain controlled. Vertigo helps teach this lesson.

I'm taking along what must be a jewel of a book for reading on this trip: Flannery O'Connor's letters—*The Habit of Being*. Also, a new small book of essays on Gladys Schmitt. Good reading guaranteed.

I wish I could guarantee myself a clear head. I do look forward to the trip, to the people I'll see, to the difficult business decision I must make. How to make the most of all this with a dizzy head? Tomorrow, no writing, even here. I'll be packing for the highly varied journey. Dress- up clothes for speaking and New York, loafing clothes for Mother's. I'm spoiled with the ease of all recent travel—mainly to nearby St. Augustine.

As much as I dislike packing and airports and waiting in check-in lines and at taxi stops, leaving Margaret is so much harder that the travel strikes me as merely a nuisance. Let's face it. Even interrupting the book would be easier if my head were not again steadily calling attention to itself.

Part Two

May 3
Back on the Island

Diaries may or may not be divided into parts, but although I have been away for only some six weeks, it was like half a lifetime and cut deeply into the continuity of these pages. I "caught myself," as old Islanders say, marking this new page as Part II. At least, for the time being, doing so will both aid my author's psyche and give some form to these pages.

My visit with Mother and Nancy and Mary Jane could not have been better. Spring was just touching the land in West Virginia, and Mother, in the main, felt well. Nance and Mary Jane were great—Nancy sticking by me, as always, when it's possible for us to be together. Truthfully, she sticks by me even when we're not together. We "did" the University of Charleston's Appalachian Festival, after some strenuous shopping for shoes for me (successful, for a change). Joyce, late because of a United Airlines strike, could spend only part of a day and one night before we flew off to New York, but we made the hours count. Mother's devotion to Joyce is a beautiful thing to watch. She wept when we said good-bye, a thing she always tries to hide from me when I leave, but I feel that this time saying good-bye to Joyce too brought on the helpless tears.

New York City was, as it always is to me, total stimulation. I vow we will go more often from now on. Any contact with publishing people sets me up and this one was almost all bright and good.

About three days into our stay there in the quaint old Royalton Hotel, Joyce developed a dreadful cold, so that she was anything but her usual entertaining self at Carolyn and Barbara Blakemore's cottage at Sag Harbor on Long Island, where we spent the weekend; but we love them both and, in spite of Joyce's illness and my severely whirling head, had a beautiful time—the four of us. Carolyn has long been one of our favorite people on earth and now there is Barbara, too. Good friends matter.

On Tuesday we flew (Joyce all but delirious with fever) to Grand Rapids, where we appeared at Zondervan's spring sales conference for most of the remainder of the week. This diary is about a novel in progress, so I am skipping details of the publishing worlds we entered, reveled in and, in a very real way, took away with us. I had seen so few of the Zondervan folk over the years, there would be no way for me to make plain here what our time together meant to me. Almost best of all was the keen interest shown in Joyce's new project for them, titled *A Book of Praises*. I caught her cold on the plane en route from New York to Michigan, so it's difficult to know which of us felt worse or which of us had a better time.

We flew home on April 12—spent over a week just sorting the stacks of mail—then Joyce and Elsie and Frances drove to Indiana for a visit with Joyce's mother, and in a day or so I went alone to St. Augustine and Hibernia—the only places I know to go when I need to get my head back together. As always, it worked. I returned to the Island on April 30, and Joyce on May 2. In fact. I've been to St. Augustine twice since our return from the still frozen North! Once, with Frances Pitts for two days, immediately after the long trip, to be interviewed for the *National Episcopalian* at Edith Cowles's lovely home by the Reverend Mr. Bob Libby, rector of Margaret Fleming's little church. The second day of that jaunt, Dena met Frances and me in Jacksonville and drove us to the home of Mr. Clement Slade, who showed his valuable collection of old stereoptican slides of both Hibernia and St. Augustine during the time of my novel. Mr. Slade is not only gracious but informed. He is convinced that in several pictures I actually looked at Margaret herself and her three daughters. I tend to agree and most notable to me is that Hibernia today, even with the big house gone, is as breathtakingly beautiful as it was when Margaret stood at the head of her long lane of crepe myrtles greeting guests from the North.

But, oh, those Victorian clothes! How the women bore up is beyond me. And minute by minute, as I work through the manuscript, I go on being grateful to my longtime and much beloved historian friend Burney Vanstory, who has done such a careful and helpful piece of work for me on What They Wore. I have depended on her for this through other novels—I needed her even more on this one. Bustles yet! Both "pointed" and "round." Women have indeed "come a long way. Baby."

During my second and much longer stay in St. Augustine, alone, I recovered completely from the long trip north and the deep cold picked up there. I feel eager to work for the remainder of this year. *If* my vertigo gets no worse. It remains a cruel, periodic annoyance.

I promised Lippincott while I was in New York that, barring some unforeseen event, I would be in the final stages of both books by February of 1980. To manage this with such an extraordinarily complex and long story to handle means working with almost no major interruptions. And so, life being life, I may not make it. But I mean to try. I am quite excited with Ed Burlingame's idea of publishing both the novel and its diary simultaneously. Writing these pages helps. Anything written down is clarified. I am not a diary keeper by nature, even though in the past I have tried to be. But these pages clarify my own life—the highs and the lows, and my capacities and limitations for handling both highs and lows as the work goes on. It is time-consuming, but I like the whole idea.

For now. Mother seems better. Ruby is home again, much improved, spring is here—almost summer on St. Simons. Not only a painted bunting sings from a tall pine as I write but a summer tanager, too—and, of course, the towhee calls constantly from the hedge.

Our beloved Sarah Edmond has the house shining, Monroe Wilson works just as diligently outside making the place look, as he declares, "like a pahk." After all those French restaurants in New York and the entertaining in Grand Rapids and nearly ten days in St. Augustine (where restaurant owners never heard of diets), I have put on only three pounds, which will quickly melt when on Monday we get back to normal.

May 7

Nothing written here for a few days, since all I've done is answer mail. Answer mail. Answer mail—and pay bills and try to figure my own finances. One letter waiting when I returned from St. Augustine was from a lady known only by correspondence, Kaethe S. Crawford. She lives in Pittsburgh, is unusually articulate and imaginative, shares my admiration for the work of Gladys Schmitt *and* has, like magic, turned into still another research lifesaver for me. I'm sure what she did was not like magic for her, so painstakingly did she work, but she is an *expert on children.* Children in general. She's been at the profession of caring for her own and other persons' children for years and has come to my rescue in such a magnificent way I'm sure Tay Hohoff is laughing in heaven. Because, at long last. I'll have an "authentic child." And not just one, but ten of them! Always, always, I am at a loss as to how to write young children—what to do with them once they're born into a novel I'm doing. That was one reason I loved *Maria*—Maria was a midwife, but had no children of her own for me to "care for." The day I had the bright idea of retaining Kaethe Crawford as my specialist on babies and small children may have been my luckiest in a long time. Yesterday, there arrived a hard-bound notebook containing at least two hundred carefully indexed, illustrated pages of "children research." She has not only given me symptoms of childhood diseases, descriptions and sketches of "baby's first steps," she has told me how to change a diaper, has written a lucid dissertation on Life in a Large Fami-

DIARY OF A NOVEL

ly—and included some favorites among children of the poems of
Robert Louis Stevenson!

I've participated in a variety of experiences in my nearly sixty-three years, but children are not among them. In fact, I almost turned down Margaret Fleming's story for the simple (to
me complex!) reason that, including her three step-children, the
spirited lady had ten all told.

Today, along with a stack of other letters, I wrote to Kaethe
Crawford and tried to thank her. I hope I succeeded.

I did not succeed, by the way, in adding anything to my
scanty store of knowledge concerning the Fleming's servants.
Phoebe Frazier sent word to me by Jane Rowley and Dorothy
Austin that she had none of the answers I sought. I already know
about Maum Betty, Phoebe's grandmother, and had begun to
write Maum Betty's mother as Maum Easter. This will stand. Her
husband's name, we know, was Pompey and Maum Betty's husband was July. So, beyond that, I am on my own.

It is late afternoon. I'm tired. But the desk is clear of unanswered mail and unpaid bills—at least until Monroe brings in
the mail this evening when he rolls up the lane with our daily
newspapers and a drugstore order. What would we do without
Monroe, whom everyone calls "Mr. Money"? He not only had the
place "lookin' like a pahk" when we returned from our long trav-
els, he had (on a ladder) scrubbed and cleaned our sign which
reads: PRIVATE ROAD—DO NOT ENTER. I don't suppose it
will make any difference to people that the sign is clear and clean.
Some will drive right past it anyway. But, at least, it can't go un-
noticed.

Forgot to mention that a friend called at 10 P.M. the other
night—a friend with a police scanner—informing me that the
police were looking for me. I called them and they were. It seems
that a young lady from another city, unable to reach me since
I have a private number, had tried the police. Now, normally, I
would no more think of returning a call like this than I would
think of flying off my upstairs balcony. For some strange reason,
this time, I did. I am glad I did. The young lady's grandmother,

gravely ill, simply wanted to send me love and to be sure I knew, before she died, how much my books had meant to her.

Sure, I complain when people track me down when I'm trying to work. But every interruption bridged by brain-bending effort, every day lost in error or confused research—all are redeemable. I confess. I'm a little scared again right now. I do not have enough time to write this long novel enjoyably as with some of the others, and so I am anxious. But this minute with every fiber of my being—just before making the terrifying plunge back into the novel itself after so long a time away—I am grateful— grateful that by profession I am a writer of books.

May 10

Intentionally, I have stayed away from this diary for three days, while taking the plunge back into Margaret's world. Words like *pain, agony, anxiety, fear* and *tension*—all come to mind. Perhaps one of the worst things that can happen to a novel in progress is to stop it cold for six weeks and allow all manner of unrelated impulses to bat- ter, soothe, stimulate, estrange one's mind. But, life can- not stop simply because one is writing a novel. The long trip, mostly happy, had to be made. And now, barring incident, I have an almost uninterrupted summer. Roughly ten days will be lost in the late autumn when I do a few—and a few only (please, God)—autographing parties for my new nonfiction book. *Leave Yourself Alone.* Beyond that, I have what every author should guarantee herself (himself)—some free time for work.

I am into Margaret Fleming's story again. Glory. Oh, I'm barely into it, but I am. I've rewritten some fourteen pages and twenty new ones. I had stopped writing on page 196. Already too long. How I will handle this I have no idea. But, today is not the day to fret and stew over that.

Today is the day to catch up here and to plow ahead with the story itself. And, I begin both with an added dimension. All along the trip and since my return, I have been reading the big new book of magnificently edited Flannery O'Connor letters—*The Habit of Being.* I have been added to by almost every line she wrote—every line that sang out in humor, wisdom, faith, even

joy, from behind her high wall of physical incapacity. Flannery
O'Connor died at thirty-eight. I wish I thought that at nearly sixty-three I had half as much sense, half as much perspective on
living with God as she had for most of her writing life. I don't
think she would have liked my books at all. In fact. I'm fairly
sure of it. We view God from difierent angles, but He would have
been a bond. I see Him in His breathtaking thrusts of creativity
and offered adequacy. Flannery's mission was to delineate evil in
the light of the Redemption. Many of my readers (others, too)
misunderstood her writing. I've heard "good Georgia ladies" de-
clare that Flannery O'Connor wrote ugly, even vulgar, books. *She
did not.* She wrote books about the evil aspect of life as it is—and
no one outwrote her. She and I could have had a million laughs
together. Her humor rang through every line—in my opinion,
God's humor. Flannery, as am I, was exhausted by every lecture
or autographing tour she ever had to make. "I have to go to a
coffee and a tea and shake innumerable paws," she wrote. "These
things are fine for the people that like them, and the people that
don't, as my mother tells me, are just peculiar." Her talent and her
courage far outreached mine, but I find comfort in that shared
peculiarity and humor.

And today, as I begin a long, long day at this typewriter, I
am added to by her "habit of being." And, dizzies or not, I am in
excellent health. Why shouldn't I work hard? Why shouldn't I, as
do all other serious writers, allow the words *pain, agony, tension,
anxiety* and *fear* to come to mind? They exist in that unfindable
part of us that creates—greatly, as did Flannery O'Connor—or
merely adequately, as with most of us. I wouldn't want to live if
I couldn't write. Neither did Flannery. I doubt that I could live
long—I hope not. She couldn't. She didn't. When she could no
longer struggle or soar with the words, she died.

I may too, far sooner than I think. But I don't think about
dying. I simply write. And if I were superstitious, which I'm not,
I wouldn't dare put these words on paper: *This morning, for the
first time since November of last year, I got out of bed with absolutely no sign of the dizzies.* The doctors say the sensation may

never return once it goes and it may also return the next day or the next year. We shall see. Today is what I have and, today, I feel like me.

Flannery O 'Connor and I also shared a confidence in prayer.

Edmund Fuller highly recommended *The Habit of Being*. I must thank Edmund. As I thank God for so much—this minute.

May 14

Time out. A writer seems never to become accustomed to this: No sooner is a new book occupying nearly all waking (and some sleeping) hours, but the galley proofs of the preceding manuscript arrive. I wrote well on the novel, I think—at least freely—on Friday. Then came the galleys for *Leave Yourself Alone*. With a sensitive cover note from my Zondervan editor, Judy Markham. Judy was not hurrying me. I hurried myself. It is far easier for me, if there is a job to be done, to do it. And so I have worked, with much pleasure, interest and profit to my own spirit, on those galleys until noon today, Monday. *Leave Yourself Alone* helped me again.

I stopped writing on the novel manuscript in a difficult place. It is rewrite, actually, as my main male character, Lewis Fleming (Margaret's future husband), is ready to leave Fort Drane in Florida, where he has been recuperating for six long months from a wound inflicted during a battle in what is now known as the Second Seminole War. It is a difficult place to stop for any length of time, since I don't yet know what to do with the chapter end- ing.

I will know eventually. Once I stop this and get to it.

May 15
End of a long workday

Except to make my daily call to our friend Ruby Wilson, who lives alone, I did nothing this morning—a blissful *nothing* at my desk—before diving back into the novel. Now, at 4:30 P.M., Lewis Fleming is no longer at Fort Drane. He is in Fernandina with Margaret (who has loved him for most of her life) and soon he will not only know of her love but will love her, too. It had better be " soon." The manuscript grows. Chapters 15 and 16 now suit me, at least structurally, but they are tricky to handle and hard to write.

This morning, Joyce was awakened in the dark at 5 A.M . by a chuck-will's-widow (not unusual, since they often call all night) and, also, by a cardinal and a tanager! We are far from being bird experts (who really is?) but, to us, for a cardinal and tanager to sing in the dark is as goofy as for our cardinals to eat azalea blossoms, which they do.

I have felt highly nervous all day—not too toppy. But so much better that I am probably only now confusing dizzies with those that come—along with the raw nerves—to every hardworking novelist.

May 16

I awakened early. During my quiet time alone, it came to me that, in spite of having written the book *Leave Yourself Alone*, I was not practicing it. Yesterday, I was struggling, painfully aware only of how hard it is to write a big novel. Well, it is hard. But, so what?

Later same day

I did it! Finally, at long last— through a part of the Second Seminole War, the burning of two family homes and a long recuperation for Lewis Fleming at Fort Drane (over two hundred pages), *I have Lewis and Margaret together*. Going to be married soon. I think it came off. I feel almost proud, even of the rough version. It is late afternoon and my head is still fine. Maybe my dizzies came from the long struggle of getting those two together. Of course, they struggled too. But no more than I. There will be other days when I'm fighting it all again—right now. I'm winging.

And I intend to enjoy. Our friend Agnes Holt is coming for dinner tonight. It is lamb chop night on the diet and she is a lamb chop woman.

May 18

Joyce found beautiful chops; I grilled them just right in our indoor kitchen fireplace, and Agnes, whose taste is superb in all things, agreed that for three Islanders who can almost never find a decent lamb chop, they were a success. Joyce's salad, as always, was superb.

The mail has been blessedly light for a whole week and, since we have guests arriving today, I notated and got off a batch for Lorrie Carlson to do. Lorrie Carlson, my Chicago right hand. Absolutely essential Lorrie. Much of my Saturday (tomorrow, mail day) will be taken up with good conversation and photography. Zondervan needs a new picture of me for *Leave Yourself Alone*, so Fm fortunate that our friends Bob and Norma Cotner had planned a weekend from the north on St. Simons. I am so sick of posing for pictures after all these years—so tired looking at myself—it helps immeasurably that the session can this time be with Bob.

He did the shot used on Maria and Joyce and I both like it. I look happy, reasonably confident and my age. Bob photographs *me*—not anyone's idealized image of me. Instinctively, he seemed to know on our first meeting that I have a good side and a funny side to my face.

Yesterday, I wrote well and covered ground. I even managed to make a few notes for what lies ahead in the novel. My people are becoming so real to me that when any living, breathing person aside from Joyce is around, I feel as though I'm in a *crowd*. In the middle of a baseball broadcast, Margaret, Lewis, the children, the servants, Louisa Fatio—all swarm around me until I have to laugh at myself. The experience is not unlike the times when Mother, Nance and Mary Jane come to mind. I feel concern, a tug at my heart, and I wonder if my people at Hibernia, too, are all right.

It is a perfect day on St. Simons Island. Pale spring light is turning to summer light and the birds are riotous. The French doors which lead to my upstairs porch are wide open and I am breathing a prayer for everyone who is, at this moment, inhaling traffic and industry fumes. Enough of this. Time for the daily big plunge back into the novel. And it does have to happen every day. A literal dive into unknown waters. My response to the daily dive is love-hate.

Monday, May 21

Our time with the Cotners was good. Bob fooled me, though! Out here at our house in the woods, with an afternoon ahead, he was fast with each shot he took—but he took ten million! I wore a pair of slacks and a denim work shirt. That, at least, allowed me to feel like me while Bob snapped. But my crazy head was crazy the whole time. Wretched circumstance for perpetual smiling.

No work, but I called Dena. She not only gives me a minimum of one or two creative opinions on some difficult spot in the novel, she seldom fails to have—right at the tip of her tongue—the answer to my question. This time, I wanted to know if present-day Aviles Street in St. Augustine, where stands the Ximenez-Fatio house, was still called Hospital Street when Margaret's friend Louisa Fatio owned and operated it as an inn for Northern visitors. Yes, it was, even though the tiny military hospital of Don Juan McQueen's time was no longer there; the name wasn't changed except quite recently when the restoration of the old city took place. And the side street, now Cadiz, was, in Louisa's time. Green Lane.

I need a day away from the novel to try to catch up on some personal mail and visit Ruby Wilson and sign some books for local stores.

Thursday, May 24

Congress seems not to be able to pass much these days, but if I had any clout in Washington, I'd try to get a bill passed for a ten-day week. There just aren't enough days. Joyce and I visited Ruby on Tuesday and, as always, she did more for us than we for her. We shopped for her first, then signed books in two stores and, in order to give me a few hours to work on mail, Joyce drove me home and then went back to do our own shopping. From two o'clock on, I managed nine letters, and the day was gone. Didn't make much of a dent in the other work piling up on my desk. My friend Nancy Goshorn laughs at my goals for myself—which are always higher than I can reach. Yesterday, I got back to the novel again and now there are eleven new pages.

Today's work is still, at this point in the morning (9 A.M.), in the area of the unknown to me. Lewis Fleming and his two motherless sons, Louis Isador ("L.I.") and George, have (as of yesterday) just returned to their much loved home, Hibernia, and experienced the shock (although they knew Indians had burned it) of seeing the once sheltering house in charred ruins. Today, I will write the scene as the three walk together down the sandy lane to the tiny cemetery to visit Augustina's grave. The boy's young, exquisite Spanish mother, Lewis's late wife, has been dead nearly four years. I must think and feel my way into their individual reactions.

Months of hard work stretch ahead on these two books, but Elsie Goodwillie, who has typed all my manuscripts since I moved long ago to the Island, is eager to begin. Last night—even with the entire rewrite still ahead and less than half the rough draft down on paper—I could tell her I was hopeful that some actual typing could begin late in the fall. Perhaps earlier on parts of this diary.

A wind is rising on the changing tide, the sky above St. Simons clouds over. That is fine with me. I love to work on a rainy day.

Wednesday, May 30

I find it hard to believe that it has been a week since I last wrote here. Not as productive a week as the one before where the novel is concerned. But those times come. I have written only seventeen pages of the novel, but I have handled business—mainly the impossible task of trying to budget my income for three or four years ahead with a brain that doesn't add or subtract easily. Tomorrow, I will have lunch with my friend Dan McCook, who is so generous as to advise me and, after a bit more negotiating, I will be back into more long days of writing. I must be.

Anne Shelander, curator of our Coastal Museum, called to nail Joyce and me down for a session of autographing in behalf of the museum for July 7. This has come to be an annual event. It is the anniversary of the opening of our restored lightkeeper's house down in the village on St. Simons. Normally, I take no dates—no speaking, no autographing, no interviews—during the writing of a novel's first draft. I break all rules' for the little museum of which I am so proud.

I am stalling here. Having been away from the novel manuscript in concentration on business and other matters for three days makes the return a near trauma. Especially when I stopped, as I did, at the end of a big section in Part II and am faced with deciding where to go next. Length is an enormous problem on this one. I must leap some time—but it must be done in a way the reader can accept without confusion.

First thing this morning, I wanted desperately to reread all I've done so far. But tomorrow the whole day is taken up with appointments which begin with a much needed haircut, so I dare not take time to reread today. I'd better take the more jarring route and *write*.

Monday, June 4

Business planning and appointments and study kept me away from my typewriter for four days. Seemed like four weeks. On the weekend, I studied research material—tried to clarify what will be happening in the novel over the next several years. There is *so much* material. Better to condense now than to be saddled with doing it all in the rewrite. A call to Mother was a happy one. My brother, Joe, is there with her and, when he's there, I can be sure Mother is laughing—at least most of the time. Today, I will begin the concentrated rereading of the 272 pages written so far of Margaret Fleming's story. At least, she is Margaret Fleming now and no longer Margaret Seton. She and Lewis are married at last.

June 5

A late start today, but for a good reason. Sarah Edmond, who keeps our house and our hearts shining, *walked* up our long, winding lane yesterday instead of scooting up in her little orange car. The automobile had broken down halfway back to our place. Joyce, bless her, put aside her own work for the entire afternoon and took Sarah to Brunswick to find another. They found one and, in the process, learned of the commendable influence of the late Colonel James Gould, about whose antecedents I wrote in my St. Simons trilogy of novels. *Lighthouse, New Moon Rising* and *The Beloved Invader.* The Goulds no longer own the Ford dealership. The Colonel's son, Jim, suggested that Sarah contact Mr. Junior Steele, a former employee. Mr. Steele recounted how, when he first went to work at Gould Motors as a very young man. Colonel James indelibly marked him with a sense of values. "Profit is one thing," Colonel James said, "but what matters most is the customer's satisfaction." Believe it or not. Junior Steele still does business by Colonel James's standards. So, Sarah will have a car on which she can depend. Thanks to Mr. Steele *and* Colonel James Gould.

We were up an hour early today. And, because we were, I could leave my doors onto the upstairs porch open until eight-thirty before the semitropical heat and steam came pouring in. I miss my open doors in summer—mainly because when they are closed, I can't hear the tanager or a single painted bunting.

Seven more pages left to reread and then I must make another plunge—into Part III.

June 7

When Joyce asked me what I wanted for my birthday, I said: "An entire month of time so free of outside pressures—business and personal—that I could actually begin writing on the novel the first thing every morning and do *nothing else.*" Since this is impossible and since life has never been known to stop or even to sweeten merely because someone living it is writing a big historical novel, I begin when I can and I plug away. I did start Part III. I am moving ahead now after some reshaping, and my interest in my people and what is happening to them is high. I managed yesterday to stop right in the middle of a scene that is already in my head, so today's writing should be easier to begin.

Called my antique furniture authority, Agnes Holt, for more furniture information—the kind of furniture Margaret might have had in her plain but comfortable house at Panama Mills, where her husband Lewis had to work as superintendent during the first years of their marriage. Agnes says much of their furniture during those years would have been plain American furniture—made on the spot of pine because pine was plentiful—and quite like an old hunt board that Joyce and I bought from Agnes when she still owned the Tabby House, an Island antique shop which has become a landmark.

Gordon Penner, the Zondervan sales representative for the area around my hometown of Charleston, West Virginia, called to share my grief and his at the sudden, useless, needless death of Elaine Howell, book buyer in Charleston, who was in that holocaust aboard the American Airlines DC-10 in Chicago last month. He and I had scheduled an autographing party with Elaine at the Diamond Department Store in Charleston early in December for *Leave Yourself Alone*. No one knows who might take her place. Filling it won't be easy. She was more than a fine book person, she was a warm, greathearted human being.

To work on the novel was—for the remainder of this day—a welcome escape into the last century with Margaret and Lewis—a quieter time when there were no DC-10s with broken bolts or cracks in their motor mountings.

June 9

Today, had he still lived on earth, my beloved father (we were two of a kind) would have been eighty-eight. Hard to comprehend. He died when he was merely four years older than I am now. What a fun man he was—is. Sometimes it requires years for the realization to come, but the sting is removed from physical death by knowing that it is not an ending but a passage into an eternal beginning. I will see him again.

I owe my baseball fanaticism to Dad and today I am a happy fan. Our young, stalwart (though fumbling) Atlanta Braves pulled a good one out last night: 11 to 6, and against Philadelphia, too—a team of seasoned pros.

A good thing because all week long I have truly strug- gled with the novel. Dozens of caring friends, such as Mae Lindsay in Virginia, Reba Spann in South Carolina, and Joyce's mother, Audry, pray for me as I work and so, now and then, I tend to feel ashamed when I struggle. Nonsense, of course. Why shouldn't I struggle? All authors do. One obstacle was resolved by a call to Dena in Jackson- ville. I needed to know where Margaret's older stepson, George Fleming, had gone to medical school back in the 1840s. There is no family record on this. When that is the case Dena and I have to use our fact-oriented imaginations. She had mentioned a school in Kentucky, where her great-grandfather graduated from medical school, but for the life of me I could not remember what it was called back then. It is, as I understand it, the University of Kentucky now. She knew at once, of course, but being Dena, she checked her facts and called back. It was then called the Transylvania Medical School.

Today, Saturday, is my day to clear up the work on my desk so far as is possible in one day. To answer the "must" letters, and sometimes, as today, to write to a few patient personal friends. Friends such as fellow writer Eileen Guder, Ellen Urquhart, Neddy Mason, Constance O 'Hara, Reba Spann, G. M. Strader, Helen Fisk and Floyd Thatcher—just writing their names causes me to wonder how or if they would like each other. They are all, in their separate ways, dear to me. And because I know they'll understand, there are times when my silences grow long.

June 14

For several days I have done almost nothing but write, write on the novel. It stands now in rough draft at page

329. I had hoped for a smoother week. I felt I would have it. I did. Christians are not superstitious, but I'm almost fearful of putting down these words: I have felt better physically than at any time since November of last year. My head seems almost back to normal. Dare I hope? Heads are strange. Under normal conditions we are not even aware of them. My near freedom from awareness of my head is so new—a matter of only five days—I am now at the exhilarating stage of being aware that I am almost *not* aware of it! To call that feeling a relief is the department of total understatement.

I began the day with a call to Dena. After research and much discussion, she has come up with a more plausible idea for Margaret's stepson's medical training than the Transylvania Medical School in Kentucky. The South Carolina Medical College at Charleston was founded in 1823 and, since young George Fleming did not go away to school until 1841, he may well have gone there. It was far more accessible to Hibernia by water. Dena has drilled me on the fact that water—the St. Johns River (which she calls "main street"), the inland waterways, etc.—were always, always used when possible in preference to hard overland travel.

I am grappling with form in the novel. The publisher does not want a long one. Long novels cost too much. I certainly understand this, but how to hold it down? Inflation cramps the style of authors, too. We just don't march, picket or strike. We're not organized—period. In fact, as a lot. I'm sure we're the most *un-* and *dis*organized folk on earth. Without the Authors Guild we would be collectively without professional representation and all sorts of things could happen to us. Even so, the Authors Guild is merely a lobby of sorts, limited in funds and influence. Those of us who are members, are, at least, kept aware by way of the Guild's superior *Bulletin* that we are not really alone. Other peculiar Americans sit at typewriters every day, too, and wrestle with the same problems. I have no complaints. I'd hate life minus the stimulation of struggle.

A full moon, laced across its orange face by pine needles, eases up over our small back marsh these mid-June nights; the gardenias are blooming in such profusion that everywhere I look in the house, Joyce has set down still another bowl of beauty. That generous Jimmie Harnsberger sent almost a bushel of huge Macon peaches, which we eat while swathed in napkins, because we run the risk of being drowned in the kind of juices that flow only out of peaches grown in Georgia. At least, Georgians are expected to say that, in spite of the fact that Georgia is no longer called The Peach State.

June 15

Not as much new manuscript as I'd hoped today. I am not comfortable (where this deadline is concerned) with less than ten pages a day—ten new pages. I did not make that goal. I did write seven and rewrote four old pages. My office is, at this point, a jungle of photocopied and typed and pencil-scrawled pages— mountains of pages, folders of research material and reference books. Only I know what each not very neat stack contains and often I lose track. In the heat of writing, I will dive at the folder marked *Margaret and Her Children*, grab out the needed page listing births, deaths, marriages, etc., use it for the scene on which I'm working—temporarily (before I forget my thought) toss it aside and, of course, forget to replace it in the *Margaret and Her Children* folder. This can create not only chaos, but loss of time, when I dive for that folder again. I long to be more organized. But I can't stop for that, I tell myself, all the while knowing what my compulsion to plunge ahead will cost me. Here I am today, looking for lost items. Self-inflicted unneeded drama.

There was a good show in our yard, too—a small, quiet wild-life performance by our tenant, Coonie. I watched him/her lope across the big front lawn and begin a search under the small grove of pear trees beside a strip of woods. There, as the coon hoped, lay a fine pear, conveniently tossed to the ground by a squirrel that adores cutting off pears just for the sheer joy of cut-ting. During lunch, Joyce informed me that this morning when she was watering azalea bushes out back, refilling bird baths and trying to scrub "bird-evidence" from the brick wall which curves around our back porch—she saw Coonie, too. "He was in back of the well house inspecting the fig tree," she said. "On his hind legs, parting the branches with his 'hands' while counting the still immature figs."

We make the same inspection every day, hoping for at least a few ripe, sun-warmed sticky fruit. Last year there was ample in-dication that figs had ripened, but only stems and tiny remnants of pink flesh remained when we went to look. Coonie obviously keeps a closer watch on the crop than we find time to do. So, we probably won't get a taste this year either. There was also a per-formance of sorts at our gate this morning. Sarah arrived to work her magic on the house just as a man and woman pulled up be-hind her in another car. Knowing we have had to lock the gate in order to discourage handshakes, luncheon invitations, autograph seekers, etc., she slipped quietly in, relocked the gate and drove down our lane toward the house. She had no more than gotten inside the back door when our intercom from the gate began its sometimes nerve-wracking buzz. I was already working upstairs. Joyce, in the kitchen, answered.

"Does Miss Price live here?" A man's pleasant voice.

"Yes."

"Is this Miss Price?"

"No, this is Joyce Blackburn."

"Well, we've been on the Island on vacation for a few days and have just managed to find her house. Does she own her own property?"

"Yes."

"How old is she?"

"Sixty-three this month." (Neither of us minds telling.)

"Oh, then is she a widow?"

"No. We're both quite happily single."

"Was she born on St. Simons Island?"

"No."

"How long has she lived here?"

"Since 1961."

"Well, what did you ladies do before you lived here?"

At that point, Joyce and Sarah, who was with her downstairs, were breaking up. Since she had been extremely accommodating so far, and since she knew I had been interrupted anyway by then (my door was open), Joyce decided she might as well try to sell a book. "You can find all your answers, sir, in a book she has written called *St. Simons Memoir*."

He ignored the book title and said, "Well, tell me. Does she own this property? How many acres?"

Who knows what else he would have asked had Joyce not brought the quiz to a polite halt? Most readers respect the Private signs on our road and gate. The exceptions sometimes demand more of me than my supply of energy allows. Usually I can shrug off their persistence. At other times, they make me feel guilt—

false guilt. The kind of guilt that needs to be handled but, because I'm grateful that they like my books—not easy to do.

Monday, June 18

I have already mentioned Kaethe Crawford, who sent me a bound notebook of wisdom about infants and children. So, when I began a scene in which Margaret Fleming was teaching her stepdaughter, Tina, how to care for a new baby in the family, I turned to Kaethe's page on diaper changing. It worked wonderfully (I sounded expert!) until I began to "use" a safety pin. My first thought was—surely, safety pins had been invented by 1842. But, to be certain, I called my good friend and researcher, Burney Vanstory, hoping she'd run across this bit of normally useless information somewhere in her vast amount of historical research. Burney didn't know, but suggested I call Marcia Hodges at our Brunswick Library. Within ten minutes, Marcia called back: The safety pin was invented in 1849! Margaret didn't have access to a safety pin that day. No pins, no snaps, no magic tape. How did women fasten diapers? How did they keep them in place on all those bare bottoms? Did they tie knots in the cloth? Uncomfortable for the baby, I'd think. Did they sew on tapes? Tape probably wasn't invented yet either! So, I suppose they simply tied knots. Unless Marcia's further digging turns up another way, that's the manner in which Margaret Fleming's babies' diapers are going to stay on. Historical research? You bet your life. (I'll be sad if final cuts force me to delete this scene!)

June 20

For two days, I heard nothing from Marcia. Bless her, today she found it—the answer to my monumental question. And I'm proud to the point of smugness. How *did* they do it? "Knots," reported Marcia. Small neat knots, I hope. Poor babies.

Yesterday and today, I have felt great—full of energy and the novel is rolling well. In fact, I'm about seventeen pages ahead of my self-made schedule. Joyce and I are toying with plans to give me a break away from the typewriter on my birthday weekend coming up. Where do I want to go? St. Augustine.

June 22
Bedtime

Today has been my birthday all day. In my date book, I wrote: My sixty-third—hurray! It was that kind of day. Every year, since Joyce and I have shared a house, I have been with Mother on my birthday. This year, our spring travel schedule sent me to Mother's in March and, for the first time, this good buddy, Joyce, celebrated My Day in person. And did she celebrate! Every time I turned around—on my typewriter, on my luncheon tray, at the bathroom basin, on my pillow at naptime—wherever I looked, there was a birthday card.

Presents began with morning coffee and continued till bedtime. When I turned down my bed just now—there was still another package! A "fun check" for sixty-three dollars, gifts, calls, flowers and fruit from thoughtful friends kept me celebrating. But, I *did* write. Just five pages, but I wrote. After all, tomorrow, continuing the celebration, we're taking off for St. Augustine for two days. Okay, maybe I do deserve a break. I have a lot of friends my age who are counting the days until they will retire. The thought sickens me. I've just set a new goal: At least eight more novels before I quit. Preferably ten.

Happy Birthday to me—and it has been. Even my head behaved.

June 29

We are back on the Island after a glorious time in the Holy City, St. Augustine. Why that tiny city casts such a good spell over me is still a mystery. I no longer visit the restorations. I know almost every board in each one. It is the high "blue-domed, Mediterranean sky," as Walter Hartridge used to say, the sounds peculiar to the town, the freedom from mail and telephone and business and house routine—the comfortable simplicity of life at the Marion Motor Lodge, heightened by an easy friendship with Stephanie and Horst, the owners, and Emma, the maid. This time there was an element of suspense: Stephanie's baby is overdue. What an ordeal! One I can't imagine putting myself through. I have enough trouble with the babies born—one after another—to Margaret Fleming.

Dena came to St. Augustine for dinner with us. Another highlight was luncheon in Jacksonville en route home at the attractive apartment of Hester and Herb Williams. Hester, mentioned often already here, is Margaret's vivacious, charming great-granddaughter, who has helped me so much. Far more than she seems to realize. Not only with hours of labor over family records, but with her continuing enthusiasm. Dena was at the Williamses' for lunch, too, along with a new friend, Fanny Pickens Inglis, a fine artist and a pure delight. Hester's luncheon was delicious, the talk stimulating, and Joyce and I discovered in Herb Williams another loyal Atlanta Braves fan!

While Dena was still in St. Augustine with us, we spent a fascinating two hours in the carefully restored Ximenez- Fatio house—in my novel, Louisa's house. Louisa is turning into one of my favorite characters and being in her house pleases me. My novel *Maria* has sent visitors by the hundreds to the St. Augustine Historical Society's prime exhibit—The Oldest House—where Maria once lived. I hope, oh, how I hope, that people who read the Margaret Fleming story will want to visit the Fatio house on Aviles Street. The Colonial Dames, who own it, have done all lovers of historical places a magnificent favor by restoring the house and gardens. Norma Lockwood met Joyce and me, along with Bob Harper, curator of Historic St. Augustine Preservation Board, for a more careful tour of the furnishings, and I am teeming to be writing about Louisa's days there—if, indeed, there is space.

Our first visit to the house earlier in the week with Dena was brightened by the company of several Florida Dames, who seem pleased that I'm doing a novel partially laid in the house on which they have labored so long so that it might be opened free to the public. Ann Jeter was there, along with Sarah Morrow, Martha Colyer, May Bobbitt and, for the first time, I met Norma Lockwood's beautiful mother, Norma Kent. I had looked forward to this meeting also with another of my Margaret's great-granddaughters, Dames president, Betty Ingle, who has also helped.

An added plum, we saw again a lady Joyce and I already loved, Mary Lewis Bliss.

My crazy vertigo is ever so slight. Especially do I notice it in a group of people, or when moving too fast in a (for me) normal burst of excitement as in the Fatio house. I am autographing on behalf of our Coastal Museum here on St. Simons on Saturday, July 7 . I wonder how I'll make out. On the whole, though, I manage fairly well. My doctor firmly believes the middle ear fluid imbalance in my case is caused by stress. But, as he wisely asks: " How can a writer write without stress?"

July 2

Now that we are back home and in the unbelievable quiet of the woods. I'm glad to be here. It is Monday morning. I have sat conferring with myself for about half an hour. What to do first? There are over one hundred unanswered letters. All the first-of-the-month bills. An unintelligible government form to get off to my accoun- tant. So *much* work piles up after even a four-day holiday. But why let it bury me? I have just decided to sort it all, snap it under a big rubber band, and go back to the novel. For me, this is progress. Never do I remember managing such a sensible decision, since for all the years of my professional life I have been unable to concentrate on writing while these other responsibilities intruded. This time, so help me. I'll do it.

July 3

Today's mail brought the complete typed inventory of furnishings in Louisa Fatio's St. Augustine house from speedy Norma Lockwood and I have filed it in my *Louisa* folder for future use. Also a call from Dena has settled once and for all the ongoing question about where young George Fleming attended medical school. From Dr. Ashby Hammond of the University of Florida, we now know that it was not Charleston, South Carolina, after all. George took his medical degree from the University of Pennsylvania. The educated guessing can stop. Dena has also found that, when he felt called to the ministry later on, George took his seminary training at Princeton. I have typed out the details of that and now it, too, is safely in the *Lewis Fleming and Sons* folder.

I have worked on research for hours on end, but I haven't actually written on the novel in nearly a week. As always, the icy plunge back into it is scary. Exciting, but scary and something I stall as long as possible. No excuse now. My head is almost comfortable and the short time away did refresh me. So—plunge.

July 6

I had one marvelous, free writing day, then a fair one— one not so free—then I was forced yesterday by an unexpected amount of desk work to stop writing. I managed (by notating and dictating) some of the most urgent letters. Today I was up at five-thirty. With such an early start, I fully expected to be five or six pages into the novel manuscript by now—eleven-thirty. I am not. Calls, calls, more business, and, although my vertigo seems less, my head whirls with dread of tackling the novel after so much other distracting "stuff." This is a day that I would be taking a tranquilizer if I took tranquilizers, which I don't. Until Margaret's story is finished, I must get some added help with the mail. Emmy Minor, our friend who owns the Clapper Rail crafts shop here, knows of a gal, Eileen Humphlett, who wants to work with me. Elsie is in the mountains for two weeks, Lorrie Carlson is in Europe. I have tried to reach Eileen, and while waiting for her line to be free, I am hereby setting down a messy diary entry which is far more typical of a writer's day than one which soars with creativity. I feel tied in a hundred knots, yet so many things are good in my life now. Even the Atlanta Braves baseball team has unbelievably won six games in a row!

A call to a charming lady named Dot Barker in St. Mary's, Georgia, brought prompt research information on my question as to whether or not George Fleming, Margaret's stepson, was indeed pastor of the Presbyterian church in St. Mary's and when. He was there from 1855 to 1858 when his name drops suddenly out of the minutes of Session meetings. Dena and I know that George was dead by 1862, when another family member wrote that George's widow, Mary Bennett Fleming, had been sent at her own request back to the North where her sympathies lay in the Civil War. If I hadn't lost so much working time on business and mail. I'd hop in the car and run down to St. Mary's to search the cemetery there for George's grave. Still, I believe that he is buried in the churchyard at Hibernia, since the family was so close. Often old markers are missing.

I will try Eileen Humphlett's number again. I do need her. The shining days in St. Augustine did wonders for me, but nothing for the new batch of unanswered mail. I'm really in trouble, but there will be a way to handle it. A rough count shows something over one hundred twenty-five now. Tomorrow will be lost to work, since we sign books at the Coastal Museum. That's always fun but I long for one solid month during which I need not go out the gate for anything. When I'm really working, I can stay inside for a whole month and not even notice.

July 7
Evening

No work on the novel today. Joyce and I signed books at the museum. As always, signing there, meeting readers face to face gave me a lift. For some reason, perhaps because I am genuinely fond of our curator, Anne Shelander, and her staff—perhaps because I'm so proud of the museum—perhaps because I'm signing at home on the Island with no travel involved—an autographing party there gives me a special boost *inside*, where I write. Readers are warm and grateful people. A humbling experience. It still amazes me how attached they are to the characters in the St. Simons trilogy. There I was, head-deep in Margaret Fleming's story, all but living at Hibernia on the St. Johns in Florida, trying with everything in me to "return" to the immediacy of the stories written so long ago about the Goulds and Anson Dodge so as to converse with those loyal readers who still remain so firmly attached to the Island people. Today, somehow, I am even more sensitized to my readers' goodwill toward me. This evening I am also in the peculiar panic which inevitably follows a busy autographing session. Panic? Yes. They stand with so much love and urgency, asking; "When is the next novel coming out?" And I am at once cheered and frightened. What if I never manage to untangle the genealogy or the history—and worse than that, what if I don't get it down on paper so these loyal readers also fall in love with Margaret and Lewis and Louisa?

Margaret Fleming is becoming so real to me, I feel overly protective of her. I sat there speaking to those standing patiently in that line at the museum, longing to interrupt their loving comments about the people in my other five novels with—"But, wait till you know Margaret Seton Fleming!" Joyce vows that my current book is always my favorite—the story and its people. It had better be or no one will read it.

I have only one bone to pick with Margaret Fleming: She had too many children! She and her Lewis gave me no consideration whatever when those babies kept coming. Will it be monotonous to readers having one baby born after another? At the party today, I blessed each copy of *Maria* before I signed it! Maria, like me, had no children at all. I look back on the writing of that book, compared to this one, as a holiday. For obvious reasons I identified with Maria more quickly, but by now, as though she were still alive on this earth and helping me, Margaret Seton Fleming is coming so clear—so close—I am almost surprised when I realize I have never actually met her. Really, talk of "liking" one character more than another is ridiculous. Readers have that right. I don't. I was drawn to them all or I could never have "lived with them" for all those years, day in and day out.

One thing is sure: *I am living* with Margaret these days. Last night, listening to my Atlanta Braves win still another game, I found my mind going to her and the birth of her somewhat slow-learning son, William. When that happens during a Braves game, I know for certain that the novel has reached the place where the creative process is probably not stoppable.

July 9

A soft, rainy day. I love a day like this. If weather preferences can be inherited, surely I received my love of rain from my mother. Rain never depresses us. It closes me into my own thoughts, by some means helps me to return after a weekend away to the book's own distinct world, to its very own "climate."

The above paragraph boded well for a quiet, concentrated writing day. Then—stuff happened. Living in the country suits me for the most part. There are also times when it seems quite insane. Too deep in the Hibernia story to notice, when I had my shower earlier, Joyce just discovered that our water conditioner system is out of salt! After her shower, the whole upstairs was infernally odorous with sulphur. Unlike some Glynn County old-timers, we have not come to relish the smell or the taste of sulphur. Lab tests show that most of the minerals known to man are present in the water that is pumped from our well. No wonder the pump, pipes, filters, even toilets get stopped up! So, novel or no novel, we have sent an SOS to Ed, our obliging Culligan man. Since he's coming, Joyce reminded me as carefully as possible, knowing how I revel in a day without a single visitor, that we might just as well call Tommy Terminix, too. We have bumble bees! Right outside my office door on the upstairs porch. We were both convinced that insects did not thrive on redwood. Bumble bees do. With secrecy and skill, a huge, fat bee is drilling through the board-and-batten wall. There is a neat pile of sawdust and, on his last trip. Tommy discovered telltale holes in some porch posts, too. Ours isn't the only Island house attacked this summer, according to Tommy, and he is at a loss to account for bumble bees switching from cedar to redwood. Could be the price we pay for having cut down most of the Island's cedars. "If you see the bee back again, call me," Tommy had said. We did. Repairmen, especially gentlemanly, pleasant ones such as Ed and Tommy, are less interruptive than a bumble bee loose in my office!

I hate poisonous sprays and am a near fanatic on not disturbing the balance of nature, but my balance must be guarded, too. Some, but not enough, work on the novel.

July 10

Hurray! Today, I was free to go straight to the novel. It is now ten minutes before noon and *fifteen new pages* are written. Fifteen pages that moved swiftly because I am mainly fictionizing.

EUGENIA PRICE

When I can fictionize—I fly. Battling my way through the complex research material on Margaret Fleming's story has just about convinced me that I may never again do another novel based on the lives of real people whose family records are known. At the completion of this one, I will have done six. And, although a few readers mention liking the fact that these were people who actually lived—whose graves, for the most part, can be found—I really think I've had it. Following stacks of family records is painfully inhibiting to the creative process. The parts most remembered, if my mail is any indication, are the fictionized parts anyway. With a fictionized story against an authentic historical background, I would fly. The fifteen pages done before noon prove it. By noon, a bigger-than-normal day's work is already finished.

After lunch, I can rest and read my current delightful biography—*Memoirs of a Victorian Gentleman* by Margaret Forster. The reading is sheer pleasure. Who would have thought I could be mad about the "Victorian gentleman," William Makepeace Thackeray? After that, with luck, I will still have time to dictate letters onto a tape for Eileen to pick up Saturday. Wouldn't it be like Christmas if, with Eileen's good help, I could find time to finish that mail stack this week? I grow increasingly fond of her.

Sky Lab is supposed to fall tomorrow. I prayed this morning for all the people with time to sit around and worry that a hunk of molten metal weighing a thousand pounds might fall on their head. Advanced technology is both wonderful and ridiculous. We can guide men to the moon and back, but an empty space station is allowed to scare nervous folk half out of their wits. I'm "right glad," as the Victorians said, to be "living" in another century.

Fifteen pages by noon. Wow!

July 12

Today's mail brought an exciting piece of news from Dena. A news item, in fact, copied from the *New York Times*, of July 1. The headline: AUCTION HOUSES SAY BOOM CONTINUES. And there, centered above the story of the phenomenal sales made by New York's famous auction houses, is a picture of Margaret Seton Fleming's beloved—and breathtakingly handsome—antique silver bowl. Anyone reading the novel around which this diary is written will know of the Seton bowl. I certainly don't intend to divulge its place in the story here, but, as though I were actually a member of Margaret's family, I am exhilarated that *her* cherished bowl—from which she and many Seton infants were christened—sold at Sotheby's for a record price! The bowl was sold by the Texas branch of the Fleming family (kind people who sent Hester Williams all the papers documenting Margaret's tragic Civil War experience) for the highest price paid ever for an item of its type—including Paul Revere's work. The *Times* called it "an outsized American silver punch bowl, circa 1799 and designed by the famous silversmith, Hugh Wishart."

Even in a black and white newspaper photograph the bowl is so magnificent I wish I could use the picture somewhere in this book. Undoubtedly not possible. Dena's *New York Times* piece has set my writer's imagination winging.

July 13

This is Friday the 13th. Sky Lab has fallen without incident. Thank God. The people who lived in those "sparsely populated" areas where it fell near Perth, Australia—real people with real names in real little towns called Esperance, Albany and Kalgoorlie—were frightened and angry. I don't blame them. At least, that's past for this time.

With so much happening in the twentieth century—Sky Lab, the president's Camp David Summit, today a PLO attack on the Egyptian Embassy in Turkey—*and* the Pittsburgh Pirates invading Atlanta Stadium tonight—I am tired, involved, confused and a touch frustrated. In the other century in which "I live," the nineteenth, there are not only rumblings of Civil War, young people to educate and marry off, there are still two more babies to come! Margaret and Lewis, dear Margaret and Lewis, had you known the burden you heaped upon my poor brain you might have had only four children besides the three who were Margaret's stepchildren—or even five. But, you had seven! And I am reeling.

My new editor. Peg Cameron, who will be with me in the final stages of both books, wondered, hopefully, on long-distance yesterday, if I might not just omit three or four children. Needless to say, I am tempted. But I have grown so close to the Fleming descendants, I want to try, at least, to stay factual on numbers of offspring. I only wish Peg could have made her suggestion to Margaret's husband, Lewis, about one hundred thirty years ago!

Peg, thank heaven, wants me to go on with the novel to the end. She would like me to finish the rough draft, then do the entire rewrite before sending it to her. She likes to work with a whole. At this stage, I prefer it that way, too. I haven't met Peg, but my late editor, Tay Hohoff, admired her, and Gladys Taber, whose editor Peg has been since Tay died, has given Peg Cameron a rosy complexion to me. After the first hello, we were friends.

In spite of the twentieth century, I have made good progress this week. Tomorrow, Saturday, I will do routine desk work, make necessary long-distance calls and watch a TV baseball game. Sunday, I will read, my favorite recreation. So far this year, I have read the Robert Kennedy biography, the Thackeray, two volumes of Virginia Woolf's letters, *This Happy Isle*, by my friend Harold Martin, *A Woman of Substance*, by Barbara Taylor Bradford—a good "read," as they say, and about four inches thick—five books for which I promised to write blurbs, *Man in Modern Fiction*, by my friend Edmund Fuller, along with his superb short novel *Flight*, Celestine Sibley's unforgettable *Jincey*, biographies of Max Perkins, Bernard Berenson and E. M. Forster—and now I am into *American Singers*, by the New Yorker jazz critic Whitney Balliett, and when I've relaxed awhile with that, I'll begin C. P. Snow's *Realists*. Of course, I am still very lonely for William Makepeace Thackeray, the *Victorian Gentleman*. There have been others. Only by reading someone else's work, am I rested.

July 17

Yesterday was the anniversary of my beautiful, gentle father's death and also my beloved Nancy Goshorn's birthday. For a long time, Nance "fooled" Mother into believing her birthday was a day later—just so Mother would not have to try to be happy on a day that still, after all these years, makes her disturbingly sad. My call to them yesterday really helped my heart. Mother is fine. I almost dare to believe—again—that my crazy middle ear imbalance is leaving me. But, oh. I'm tired. Not physi- cally. Psychically. In fact, first thing this morning, I bent Joyce's patient ear for an hour with my inner turmoil. For once, there is no—absolutely no outward reason for it. These times of near total frustration in the making of a big novel simply come—over and over again. How can I be so self-deceived as to think they won't happen yet again? And again? I love writing novels and I hate it. For the first time, I understand a love-hate relationship. And, if this diary has any value, perhaps it is to give me the needed hand-up on days like this when I'm down-right ashamed to feel scared of my work. Writing it down here releases something. Another benefit could be that it may—I pray it will—prove to some of my readers that, at times, I'm a weak, frightened, faulty, out-of-control human being just like anyone else. If something I've written has helped a reader, I am grateful—God knows that. But there is often the danger that the person who has been helped will put me on some kind of lofty pedestal. Let me in, people! I'm in an agony of humanity today.

Joyce says everything I say about my fear of disappointing my readers, my fear of not doing justice to the novel—indicates nothing beyond tiredness. She may be right. But the book has to be done. I have a contract. I need the money. My responsibilities are heavy. And, anyway, I'm so into the story, I'd be in a far worse agony if I took time off.

Someday, someday, perhaps I will be able to take all the time I really need to write a novel. I would never procrastinate. I love doing them too much. But, at this stage in my life I simply can't afford a slow, steady pace. There is always the problem (quite understandable) that publishers want their money, too. The house of Lippincott makes nothing until I'm finished.

I am also worried about the growing length, which will increase the novel's cost. I am in sympathy with all the economic realities. And the war with my psyche.

117

The sun is shining—clear, burning Island sun. Even our long-vanished mockingbird. Snoopy, has returned. Other birds are, at least, somewhat predictable. Snoopy vanishes for weeks at a time and we grieve. But more often than my antisuperstitious mind wants to admit, *he returns just when I need him most.*

No explanation for Snoopy. None is needed. Nor, actually, is one needed for my temporarily darkened thoughts. God knows I'm not depressed often.

July 19

About midafternoon yesterday, I came to the relieving and also difficult conclusion that I must stop writing and take at least a day to study. It is time in the manuscript to build a huge house, "birth" one more child, marry off another, wade into the Civil War, both politically and emotionally—all while I try to convince myself that by some means I will one day finish the rough. What I wouldn't give for a cottage on fifty acres by myself! This morning, in a good frame of mind, I got up to work. There were two long calls re an immediate community crisis. Plans have been made public for hundreds of new housing units, a motel, shops, marina—which will ring Christ Church and Fort Frederica National Monument! The development epidemic on St. Simons Island is virulent. This morning, a biography and letter must go off to a girl doing a term paper on me, and as usual, although I received her request only   yesterday, she needs it now. The house is being cleaned of necessity—the Hoover roars. Two friends called. A lady climbed over our gate and wandered up the lane—just wanting to shake my hand. Of course, there is a neat sign on the gate which reads: *Uninvited guests cannot be received. Thank you for respecting our privacy.*

It is one o'clock. Finally quiet, but how to get back into the novel? I'll call Dena in Jacksonville and Jackie Bearden in St. Augustine. Both will help solve my current Civil War research problems and both are so "with me," I fully expect my poor, scrambled brain to unscramble. I am *not* on top of my story now. The story is smack on top of me.

July 23

During the weekend just past, still more calls about the planned horrendous development of the historic end of the Island—Frederica, where I live. In fact, some of my black depression of last week—panic that I would not make my deadline—had to be caused by those calls. I've accepted growth on St. Simons. I no longer become ill at the thought of Frederica being changed, within reason, but there are always meetings connected with any community action and Joyce and I are expected to attend. I missed a deadline once before because of this very same threat. Our efforts were successful then, but I dare not miss my current deadline. There are meetings I should attend. I am not going. I must risk being misunderstood on every front until the rough draft is finished. I marvel that Joyce remains so staunchly understanding and protective of me. Once the complex story is down on paper—even before the long rewrite begins—I can ease up a little. Can be interrupted without such devastating results. But that will be at least the end of August. Well, I've written in other books that one mark of true maturity is the willingness to be misunderstood. I'm willing.

Today, at least, most of my panic is gone. Books do get written. A friend innocently drove me up the wall by saying, "Oh, chin up! you always make it. You've done it so often before. I can't believe *you* really get scared." I wanted to burst into tears, a thing I don't do easily. At this point in Margaret's overpopulated story, the precedent of five other published novels is no help at all. Not an iota of help, since no two present the same problems. Similar emotional reactions in me, yes. There are at least ten panic periods survived during the writing of each one. With Margaret's story (I *do* wish I could find a title!), the one overriding and continuing problem is the *number of children*. Had she given birth to only a few, the story would almost write itself. But she didn't. And when one is following a family story about real people, that settles that. How, for example, could I just omit Hester Williams's grandfather, Frank? Or Dorothy Austin's father, Frederic? Tissie and Belle could be omitted, since they left no children, but I need Belle for my ending. Maggie cannot be omitted as though she were never born because she is Margaret's mainstay *and* the cause of Margaret's near collapse at the end. I could omit poor William, who was slow-witted, but he is one of the most tempting characters to a writer. And so it goes.

In spite of the fact that my Atlanta Braves lost three one-run games over the weekend and President Jimmy Carter is being talked and written about as though he is a moron, I am determined that nothing will distract me, nothing hold me back this week. Once I can begin the rewrite, I know I'll find ghastly errors in what I've done during these past months when my head scarcely seemed attached. Novels do, in the final analysis, come out of an author's head. Better not dwell on that.

My current personal reading is C. P. Snow's *Realists*. In the section on Balzac, one line stopped me: "...his literary achievement moved smoothly to its peak, though nothing else in his life moved smoothly." Conversely, my life moves along with relative smoothness, while my writing goes poorly—so poorly I despair at times. Still, a friend wrote last week: "I have your letters to prove what I am about to say: In every single one of the other novels, you have despaired because your writing was going so poorly." Good grief!

Novelists must be very monotonous friends. The best cure for the writing and for me is—more work. Right now.

July 30

I have intentionally allowed a week to pass without mak- ing an entry in these pages. I was growing repetitious: Too much like real daily life to make good reading. I was boring myself. Now? Improvement. My perspective has lifted. Within a few more days of familiarizing myself with vast amounts of unstudied research material, I feel as though I can plow straight to The End. Part of the problem is that one is into a book over a period of so many months; the research material keeps growing and I fell into an easy trap: I simply *forgot* that I had familiarized myself in depth with only the first two-thirds of the material.

Last night, regretfully (although it is the kind of book one rereads) I finished C. P. Snow's *Realists*. I sighed with envy as he described the way Marcel Proust assembled the boxes of manuscript for his enormous novel Swann's Way. I had already spent my period of awe at Snow's narrative about the writing of *The Brothers Karamazov* (Dostoevsky) and *War and Peace* (Tolstoy). I am not, by the wildest stretch of anyone's imagination, in the exalted realm of Proust, Tolstoy or Dostoevsky, but another passage of Snow's near the end of the book comforted me. He declares that all writers—even the great ones—are people, and being people, they are people with problems. In a cogent Epilogue, he writes: "These were great writers; but great writers are also writers, and suffer from the occupational hazards and weaknesses of their profession. We have seen them behaving exactly like other writers, having to shape their work to fit the publishing needs of their time, often doing work they shouldn't have done because of need for money, and sometimes behaving with distinguished unscrupulousness."

I add: sometimes behaving with downright panic and fear and complaints. Bellyaching at having to do the agonizing thing they love most in all the world. Seeming to shut out everything but the work in progress. Seeming to? *Doing it.* After telling of the wild grief of Proust following the death of one of his lovers. Snow writes some lines which I not only understood, but which relieved me to no end: ". . . racked by misery as dark as when his mother died, Proust was showing untiring energy [in the midst of the new grief], perseverance, acumen about getting his first volume published. In a sense the novel was inseparable from his innermost self, as no experience was, neither love nor grief. This may make him appear less than human, but it has been true of writers nearer the mainstream of existence than he was capable of. Think of Conrad, writing away in creative fervor while his son was dying in a room close by."

Well, I've worked—not always well, but compulsively— when Joyce has been ill "in a room close by." I wrote steadily as soon as I returned to my desk from my father's funeral. I worked well and hard and energetically today while Joyce is at our local hospital sitting with our beloved Elsie Goodwillie, who is undergoing risky surgery. Elsie not only handles my manuscripts in a most singular way, she is my close friend. And yet I work. With near "untiring energy."

And I am growing freer and freer of a false guilt I've carried all these years when I didn't "act Christian" but worked instead. Nonsense. I am being my best Christian self when I work. True, my best isn't good enough, but then whose best is? Could I be—at long, long last—at my age, learning something about myself which God and probably my friends have longed for me to learn for years? I used to look at the formidable stack of unanswered letters and half drown in a swamp of false guilt for my lack of "Christianity." Now, I look at them, sometimes I even grin, and almost always I say—"Well, I'll get to them someday."

I've come by this new (still familiar) freedom during the writing of these pages, so far as I can see.

Perhaps when I learn fully how to take one day at a time and handle what the hours will allow, my head will straighten up and stay that way.

Nothing is more a part of my "innermost self" than Margaret Fleming's story. From now until it is finished, all else will, in some way at least, be extraneous. Selfish? As C. P. Snow wrote, "less than human"? All right. So I'm selfish and less than human because this kind of concentration is absolutely necessary if one is not to write disconnected superficialities. Granted, my books are considered by the more esoteric critics as sentimental, magnolia-scented fluff. They're not considered that by my readers and I find my readers intelligent, widely read and honest enough to admit liking a good yarn about believable people who trust God and find no need to "hunt for Mr. Goodbar."

July 31

Tuesday is one of my two freest workdays of the week. The house is quiet—no one comes to clean, or mow the lawn under my windows, I don't make my midweek (long, long) long-distance call to Mother until tomorrow. Joyce is with Elsie at the hospital. There is a full day of Margaret Fleming ahead. And it will begin with some digging into the right way to move into the Civil War.

Joyce and I had a good laugh at breakfast. She is at work on a fascinating compilation and is searching about fifty or sixty books at once in her office. She can almost not maneuver her way around the stacks to reach her desk! I sit here glancing around at my cluttered office—aware that I'll spend a total of at least two hours during this day *hunting* for photocopied sheets which I know are here because I used them yesterday, but which, dur- ing the night as I slept, moved themselves to devilishly obscure spots. Just the mechanics of this novel overwhelm me some days. I can spend half an hour leafing back through this now huge stack of manuscript, fearful that in the swamp of new material I've forgot- ten whether or not one of Margaret's children has even been de- scribed—or, heart pounding for fear I've forgotten to "get in" the Abolitionists in time for Margaret and Lewis to have a conversa- tion about them. Another half hour can go down the drain while I hunt back through two hundred or three hundred pages to see how recently or how long ago I gave the reader a "report" on how the Fleming son George and his new wife are doing. Oh well, this is Tuesday—that good, free day—John Brown and his sons are fighting against slavery in the Kansas Territory, and my fam- ily, served by both free and enslaved Negroes, must register their reactions to all this. Floridians were very divided on the slavery issue. After all, their livelihood—even then—depended in large part on Northern tourists. It is a fascinating period in history and a look at the Civil War from a unique state with "mixed mo- tives." Floridians were, by no means, all rabid anti-Union folk.

August 2

It is 11:30 A.M. and I am just getting to work. This, in spite of the fact that I was up early in order to write three letters explain- ing to three different readers who want to take me to lunch that I can't leave Margaret Seton Fleming. I try to refuse lovingly.

With Joyce at the hospital with Elsie yesterday, I man- aged eleven new pages between trips up and down the stairs to con- fer with the pump repair man, a most likable fellow, who knows about wells and the eccentricities of our water. It was fine for my shower yesterday morning. Not for Joyce's. No water. Pressure gone. Barney, the pump man, fixed it, drove half a mile down Frederica Road and off went the water again while I was washing the breakfast dishes. I called him back. He came, worked his magic once more. Water flowed until Joyce started to prepare our dinner last night. Barney was here at nine-thirty this morning and at last we have running water again. Who thanks God that water (however contaminated) flows from a faucet when it is turned on? I do, today at least. Also, it kept me in the mood of the novel. After all, Margaret Fleming had to supply pitchers of water for thirty Yankee guests! She had no faucets.

There have been calls to and from the hospital, numerous calls from friends concerned about our beloved Elsie—still very ill. Will I be able to settle down and write? Joyce has gone again to be with Elsie when she returns to her room from the *second* surgery this week. Again, I remind myself— God is in charge. He is.

August 3

I did settle down and I worked well. In fact, the past days have been productive. I'm working on largely fictionized scenes, dialogue, transitions based on family and historical fact. I am literally hooked on southeast coastal history and must constantly keep myself reminded that no matter how interesting an event is to me, if it doesn't move along Margaret Fleming's story—forget it.

Of particular interest to me is divining what her attitude must have been toward her handsome, dashing, military-minded son, Seton. If a good mother can be said to have a favorite—Seton was Margaret's. Research and reading convince me that both Margaret and Lewis Fleming were moderates in the Civil War. Lewis fought in the Second Seminole War and had the typical man-of-his-period view toward courage in battle. Margaret, I believe, truly understood that, but I am convinced that she simply *hated all war*. That she could *not* have brought herself to the place of loathing Yankees. She feared for her sons' safety—all four fought—but she prayed, too, for the sons of Yankee mothers at whom her own boys might shoot. Just as she prayed for Seton and Frank and Frederic and William. She watched breathlessly each day for a letter from Seton, fighting in Virginia. And yet, today, it struck me that, although she welcomed every word he wrote, her heart must have sickened that, judging from his actual letters to which I have access, this loving, attractive, sensitive lad wrote *mainly* of the gory details of killing. She understood it because she understood Seton, a Rebel hothead. He had inherited some of her own impetuosity. But she deplored to the depths of her being that the necessity to kill might scar him. This can all be strengthened in the rewrite. How I do count on that rewrite!

August 6

Under every paragraph, under every newly formed concept—under all activity—runs our deep concern over Elsie, still in the hospital. I drove to Brunswick to see her on Saturday. Such a great, buoyant, lovable human being. Jimmie Harnsberger wired a huge bouquet of daisies for us to take to Elsie as if from us. There are times when true, undemanding, totally giving friendship overwhelms the heart. Always, it overwhelms the mind.

Another shining example of this kind of caring: Dena, upon learning of new research needs from me yesterday, remembered two pertinent books: one including the actual letters from Margaret Fleming's sons during the Civil

War; another, a cogent history of the war *in Florida*—so different from the other states of the Confederacy. And, realizing my urgent need, hopped in her little blue Pacer yesterday (Sunday) and with our friends Bill and Mary Lewis Bliss, drove the seventy miles from Jacksonville with the books! At some point since our Friday call, she had also typed out a dozen or so added pages of needed facts. What I would have done without her on this, the most difficult novel to date, I still dare not think.

We shared our Sunday diet luncheon—and, hungry. I'm sure, the three drove off with our predictable afternoon storm brewing. From that moment—about 3 P.M.—until midnight, I studied! The material Dena brought is so exciting I didn't even touch the Sunday papers. Sunday is my only day not to work. This week I did and happily. I "dug" all day in the new books. I will go on digging tomorrow. Men who used to dig ditches with shovels or some such now have machines. Writers of historical novels still don't. I think I'm glad.

August 8

There has been little time to write in these pages during the early part of this week. I've done well, considering what has happened to Elsie, to stay with the novel. I did stay with it, thanks to Joyce, who is almost living at Brunswick Hospital. On Monday, we learned that Elsie was scheduled for lung surgery Tuesday morning. Monday night I joined Joyce and Elsie at the hospital and only Christians could or would even try to believe the good laughs, good sense and downright fun we had together! Elsie said, "If I wake up here and see you gals, we'll go on having a ball like always. If I wake up in heaven, I'll see God and Walter." Walter, her husband, always a lively member of every "party," died four years ago. Until visiting hours ended at eight-thirty, we shared that rare kind of light-filled love and certainty in God which His children *can* experience.

The surgery, with our good friend, Dr. E. R. Jennings, went well the next morning and now Elsie is in the intensive care unit. Joyce drove all the way from our north end of the Island to Brunswick for the allotted five-minute visit in intensive care last evening and thinks Elsie knew her. Dr. Jennings just called and, considering the seriousness of the surgery, she is doing extremely well. One of the last things Elsie said to me was, "Now, don't let this dumb thing upset you. Keep going on those two books!"

I am. With enormous thanks in my heart for concentration "in the midst of." Today, in the novel, I am attempting to move swiftly into the buildup to the Civil War. I must make it clear and simple. It is not simple, but I must be selective and get it down so clearly that the facts are integrated into the story itself. It is not easy to sort out. Especially to write it so that my research doesn't *show*. Strong Unionists remained in Florida after secession. Of course, strong Rebels as well. I believe Margaret and Lewis to have been *un-fiery* Confederates, who hated the war and who tried to keep their emotional balance. Margaret in particular. Lewis died in 1862, leaving her to face the horror alone with her daughters, since all four of her sons fought—even retarded William at age sixteen. Lewis died of what the family records call "a congestive chill." The records say that he died "within a few hours." Along with all our other calls coming in and going out re Elsie's surgery today, I checked with our "family doctor," Bill Hitt. What is a "congestive chill" in today's medical understanding? Of course, I wouldn't use a contemporary term, but I need to know symptoms. Probably a congestive heart, but Dr. Hitt suggests that I also consult with some older doctors.

Right now, I must place Margaret's slow son, William, in one of the guerrilla bands that sniped at Yankee gunboats from the tops of trees along the St. Johns. Dena could not find William Fleming listed among those who were actually members of the Confederate forces.

August 10

Today, we're lyrical! Our dear Elsie—two days before we dared expect it—is out of intensive care and into a regular room. Her surgery has kept me running on two separate tracks this week. My deep concern for her, which is the imrnediate reality of life here, but just as real to me: life on the St. Johns River in the 1860s with Margaret and Lewis and their family at the outset of the Civil War. My heart has been pulled nearly apart. Brain, too. I have suffered with Elsie, and with Joyce attending her—and with Margaret and Lewis and their wildly disrupted lives. Can't pretend I'm bored, at least. Not for a single minute.

I'm running out of space in my office for the stacks of research material from Dena and Hester—plus (at the moment) five separate history books all open to marked pages. Three reside, opened, on my typewriter table and seem to move on their own. I keep typing them off into my waste basket. No room on the desk. I wonder if I dare actually put this on paper— but I am beginning to see light these days. If I get any sort of break in the interruption department, I could—I *could* finish the rough draft in ten days! Ten working days, that is. The mail stack is so old now, ten more days can't matter.

Joyce laughed at me last night and it helped. We were reading in the living room and suddenly I said: "I *know* I've gotten way off the track in this novel! There's just too much dialogue." This is when she laughed. "Well, good," she said. "You said that about *Maria* in the rough draft, too, and, in my opinion, that book has amazing balance between dialogue and narration.' I hope she's right. She usually is.

August 13

Saturday was—for this period—a strange but good day. At the top of the page in my date book, I wrote: A Very Long Day Away From Margaret and Lewis. It was. But I am free now to begin this week with a clear conscience. We had lunch with friends whom we hadn't seen in weeks, we visited Elsie in the hospital and Ruby Wilson at her home, did the grocery shopping, other errands, I signed fifty books for a gift shop called Pelican's Perch, then home for dinner. Someone said of the day, "Well, you needed the change." Perhaps. I flare a little inside when friends urge me to stop working so hard. They may be right. But, since I never relax away from my novel people, maybe they're wrong and I'm right.

Sarah Plemmons came for dinner—Joyce's excellent curried chicken—and Sarah, bless her, brought us bags of fresh vegetables from the "curb market," which I've never seen and, please God, will never have to see. I loathe shopping.

Yesterday, Sunday, a good laugh with Dena (there is always a good laugh with Dena!). I called her in Jacksonville especially to tell her that I thought she should know that throughout the weekend she was a resident of a city still in the possession of Confederate forces.

This is what happened and it illustrates clearly how confused an author's mind can get in the midst of sorting out research, while trying to keep characterizations vivid and drama building. Total confusion can take over even when the author knows exactly what did happen: On Friday, as Joyce and I had morning coffee, I explained that the first thing I had to do that day was to surrender Fernandina, Jacksonville and St. Augustine to the Yankees. All three towns surrendered without a shot fired in March of 1862. I had it absolutely straight. What did I end up doing once I rolled a sheet of paper into my typewriter? I went sailing blithely into the battle experiences of Margaret's sons! By some quirk, I allowed Margaret's anxieties to push out of my mind the surrender of those cities. Before I began to write, I picked up those marvelous letters Dena brought written from the Virginia battlefield and so went headlong into Seton's accounts of battles. Now, that sequence will, of course, be in the book. It happened. But—it didn't happen until July and those towns were surrendered in March. That, of course, left Dena, who lives in Jacksonville, in a Confederate-occupied city for the entire weekend! The same for the citizens of Fernandina and St. Augustine. We'll get a lot of mileage out of that goof and it's typical.

Sorry to end this entry. It means I have to find out now what I really did write on Friday and correct it. Oh well. With any luck, I will be nearer the end of the rough draft at this time next week. Probably about fifty pages nearer. I'm straining at the bit these days for the end of the rough. Eager for the rewrite to begin. The smooth, as Pamela Frankau called it. One can hope, at least, that the rewritten stack of pages will be smoother. And *fewer* in number.

August 14

I needed the relaxtion of last evening—dinner with our longtime and much loved friend Jingle Davis and Bill Morehead, whom I met for the first time—and loved on sight. They are both writers and understood, along with Joyce, to the point of laughing at me with compassion at just the right times, because I was already grieving over what lies ahead for me today: *Margaret's beloved Lewis will die.* It is 11 A.M. now. I have written up to that dreaded moment. I must not only stay cool enough to handle the mechanics of the scene, I must handle my own emotions, too. My people on the St. Johns are, right now, far more real to me than anyone else I know. Well, Lewis has to die. Might just as well get to it.

August 15

Lewis Fleming died yesterday at my typewriter at about 4 P.M. Joyce, of course, was not here. She has gone daily during these two weeks to check on Elsie at the hospital in Brunswick. I desperately needed both solace and celebration. Solace, because I loved Lewis. Because I love Margaret. Interesting—in that sentence, I quite unconsciously used the past tense, *loved*, for Lewis. The present tense, love, for Margaret. That's how real they are for me as I write. And now, dear Lewis is dead. And Margaret, like me, is full of grief. I also needed celebration because I wrote well through this difficult scene, felt all right and had my old, normal energy back. I didn't even want to quit working after five o'clock. I could have kept on through the evening. But, I did quit—when in one hour the telephone rang nine times: "We are here on vacation. When can we see you?" "How is Elsie Goodwillie?" "Can you do an autographing party in my store for your new book this fall?" The callers were cordial, our conversations pleasant, but I am not living—just hanging on by my fingernails to life in the twentieth century. And I like it this way! Readers write that they become so involved in one novel or another, they forget to prepare dinner, make beds, make phone calls, etc. Well, multiply that by infinity and you have some idea of how hard it is for the author to cope with daily life.

What did I do for solace and celebration? I called Dena.

What else? She comforted me over Lewis's death, exclaimed joyously because of the return of my energy, the apparent clearing of my head after all these months—and before we hung up, I found myself actually reading aloud the portion about Margaret's reaction to the sudden loss of Lewis, so much a part of her. After I began reading, I almost felt panic. I had not read one word of those eighteen pages of the death scene. What if it bogged down and Dena thought it dreadful? What if I thought it dreadful? We didn't. Her response: "I'm crying." My response—"I'm really writing again with the old drive and joy."

That was to be the last line of today's entry, but Joyce just walked into my office with a shocker. Christ Church Frederica around the bends in the road from our house and the setting for much of my St. Simons trilogy of novels—was broken into. Joyce is trying now to find out for our friends Teensie Bradshaw and Elsie Permar, coeditors of *The Islander*, the extent of the damage. One rumor: A lovely old stained-glass window was broken and a cross stolen. Cult ritual, including black candles lit on cemetery tombstones, chicken sacrifices in some form of devil worship, has gone on in the churchyard for some time. Our own security man saw this taking place. But until last night, the church itself had not been harmed. I could stop and drive over there to find out. I'm not sure I want to. Far better for me to return to the St. Johns River and Hibernia. Far better many days to escape the twentieth century altogether.

August 16

At the end of the day yesterday, Kitty Grider, one of the Gould descendants, whose family story is told in my St. Simons trilogy, called to say that Horace Bunch Gould II, of Jacksonville, my beloved friend to whom I dedicated *New Moon Rising*, has suffered a severe stroke. Horace has not lived fully since the day we buried his Emmy in the churchyard at Frederica. Our hearts are heavy. A much loved gentleman. A true southern gentleman, whose kind heart and gracious ways made him very spe- cial to me. So many of the older members of the Gould family he already in the Christ Churchyard. Our Island family. I will be glad for Horace to be free and back with Emmy and his ancestors, but I will know another empty place in my life. I am devoted to him.

And Margaret Seton Fleming is about to be chased by the Yankees from her beautiful house—on foot out into the dark woods. The story quickens now and my problem of length increases. Everything hangs on the rewrite—but then it always does.

August 17

Joyce has driven to the mainland to bring Elsie home from the hospital far sooner than anyone dreamed. I try not to think about it—but now and then the strange apprehension comes that, for the first time since we moved to St. Simons Island nearly twenty years ago, Elsie might not be up to typing these manuscripts. But that problem must be settled at a future date.

Today's entry here is for recording just this one funny thing and then to work on the novel. Yesterday's mail brought an amusing and always happily received letter from my "pen pal," the fine, provocative and well-loved author Gladys Taber, in which she related two marvelous stories about her adventures (and misadventures) with her vast letter-writing public. Authors do get some strange mail—strange requests, etc. Both Gladys and I would hate receiving even one letter less. She was not complaining and, like me, she faithfully answers each one by some means and at some point. Now and then we share an especially colorful request we've received. I treated myself to a quick reply to Gladys today before beginning this entry. I had a lulu for her: Yesterday, I received a letter from a woman who collects buttons! She frames and mounts them to hang on her wall. She already has quite a collection, it seems—among them buttons from a dress worn by Vivien Leigh. Now, she wants two of my favorites. Joyce suggested that I write her a note saying that " I need all my buttons." I thought, from the warm tone of her letter, that she might laugh if I said, "I lost my buttons." The truth is that I've never had a favorite button in my life, but I shall dig up a couple of shirt buttons. I'm happiest in shirts and that gives shirt buttons a slight edge in my affections. I do appreciate that she took time to write me and one of these days she will get her buttons. She even bothered to tell me that I would have to get a padded mailer in which to send them. Fortunately, I have a supply of small padded mailers, purchased for sending tapes of dictated letters to Lorrie Carlson in Chicago. Once, in an airport limousine, a lady asked me to autograph her new purse. I did. Another time, after a speaking date, a gentleman asked me to sign his forearm. I did. Buttons are a first for me. Although, another reader did send me an old- fashioned wooden mustard paddle to autograph and return. I signed it and now it is in her "spoon collection."

August 20

Saturday, my head was so good I didn't know I had one, which is as it should be. Then—whammo. Sunday, that old uncertain, vibrating, spacy feeling returned. Not severe, but depressing. This week is very key to the winding up of the novel. More than anything, I need to feel well. Still, I've learned that one can work though *not* feeling well. There is no thought of not working. But, since everything from this point on depends upon my instincts in structuring the remainder of the story, I need those instincts to be unhampered.

August is not a good time to be in such a bind with a big novel. "Yankees" invade the Island in droves and a few are personal friends. I literally pray for understanding of my need right now not to have engagements—even pleasant ones. Perhaps I'm not quite as willing to be misunderstood as I like to think I am, or I wouldn't mention it here again.

I do feel better today—Monday—and today is what I have. Unless something interesting beyond what will happen to Margaret happens to me, I don't plan to write much in these pages this week. I am going to do my level best to concentrate only on the novel. The old familiar mix of downright stage fright and good anticipation grips me this morning. One thing is sure: The passing of the next few days will automatically bring the novel's first draft finally to an end. The story, at least, will be down on paper. This will be automatic because, barring catastrophe, head good or bad, I mean to be at this type-writer all week adding at least ten new pages a day.

August 21

Forget what I wrote yesterday. Here I am back in these pages! Writing here has become a salutary habit. I find it propels me into the novel itself and at least somewhat focuses my mind when so many other things intervene, as today. Seeing me grow more and more uptight as the morning progressed, Joyce told of a funny scene that she witnessed yesterday and it did make me laugh. In a local shop, she overheard one shopkeeper say to another: "The way these tourists bother us, it's no wonder people hate Eugenia Price!" Let me say quickly that most of our Island business friends are just that—friends. They are plagued by requests for my unlisted telephone number and directions to my house, but cover for me good-naturedly. I'm embarrassed much of the time because the Island business people *are* my friends. Most give me a hand-up in my embarrassment. That one shopkeeper had simply had it and I certainly understand. I do a lot of sincere apologizing, both to readers who are kind enough to want to take me to lunch and to the shopkeepers.

Attempting to write courteous refusals to six invitations to lunch right when Margaret needs me so much has driven me first to these pages instead of the novel today. The people who invite me are almost always arriving within a few days. I can't hold their letters until later.

Of course, I wake up with only the novel on my mind. Unfortunately, I built my office into my house and there is a telephone—and yesterday's mail on the same desk from which I write books. I imagine this all sounds like melodramatic hogwash, but today Fm like a person adjusting emotions after a kind of nightmare. I move on three levels: My personal life, the outside work and the novel. Only one is real to me. The novel. My novel people at this crucial point are all I can cope with. Yesterday, in fact, in a somewhat distracted state, I *forgot* to anchor a Yankee gunboat in the St. Johns in front of Hibernia and so have to rewrite about seven pages.

This morning, early, Joyce said, "Don't forget to call about the Lewis dates." Said I blankly: "But Lewis is dead!" When she began to laugh, I still looked bewildered.

"Darling," she said, "Frank Lewis. The company in Texas that sells those delicious Medjool dates!"

August 23
In my novel, *New Moon Rising*, the dedication reads:

To My Valued Friend,
Commander Horace Bunch Gould II.

Horace is gone.

As with the deaths of the other Goulds in the past years, Kitty Grider, his niece, called us within minutes after she heard. I wish I thought the Goulds—the living ones—knew for certain what their continuing inclusion of Joyce and me in the family circle means to us. We will bury Horace beside his beloved Emmy in Christ Churchyard tomorrow at 10 A.M.

Today, I have been hard at work on Dena's magnificent but, to me, mysterious maps and Pat Wickman's fine research on Civil War hospitals. Margaret nursed in General Hospital in Lake City, Florida.

Hope to get in a big day—unlike yesterday when business calls and letters blocked any concentrated work until 1 P.M. I did manage ten new pages, though, by skipping my prescribed rest period. Maybe—just maybe, after some time spent with our dear Goulds after the funeral services tomorrow I can again skip the rest time and do another few pages. Saturday is filled with uncancellable appointments. Sunday, my favorite day just to enjoy my home and read, may turn into a workday this week. The pressure is my own doing. I am too near the end to allow three whole days to pass without time spent with Margaret.

Erskine Caldwell once said: "I think it must be remembered that a writer [novelist] is a simple-minded person to begin with and go on that basis. He's not a great mind, he's not a great thinker, he's not a great philosopher, he's a story-teller."

True, true. But a story is a living entity. It dies in the novelist's mind if too much time is spent away from it. If too many distractions occur. Writers really are, after all, "simple-minded."

August 24

Up at five this morning to study my research material in the early quiet, even before conversation with Joyce. Good thing! After a long, stimulating, helpful telephone conversation with my absolutely essential Dena Snodgrass last night, I *accidentally* left on my desk the two-page report she had written for me, headed: Civil War in Jacksonville and on the St. Johns. Had I not been careless and hurried back downstairs to play records with Joyce after Dena and I talked, I might have put that sheet of paper away in a folder and never found it again!

There it was—smack in the center of my desk at five this morning—and when I read it, I found still another dramatic sequence which *must not be left out*. Three Yankee gunboats were blown up at Mandarin Point—near enough to Hibernia so that Margaret and her girls would surely have heard the explosion. Joyce came sleepily into my room about seven and almost before her eyes were open, I shouted: "Honey, three gunboats were torpedoed and I almost missed it!"

She blinked, smiled and said foggily: "Three torpedoes? How marvelous! I know how happy that makes you!"

I am writing this near dinnertime—the end of a long day of work and emotion. We said good-bye this morning to Horace Bunch Gould. What a beautiful man he was—is. I sat there, as I've sat at the services of so many older Island friends and thanked God for every touch from the life of Horace. These days one seldom uses the word *noble*, but it belongs to him in a unique way. Only his brother. Potter, is still here. But he is alertly and strongly here. Potter and I held hands at the graveside while he said: "Genie, I wish you could write something about him. You'd know how to do it." My heart moved. I felt it. I have written three novels about the Gould family. I have never known more affectionate folk. Nieces and nephews wept for Horace today. That is no longer usual. The Goulds are not "usual" people. During the writing of the St. Simons trilogy, telephone calls from Horace were always buoying experiences for me. He believed in what I was trying to do in my novels. His faith in me meant more than he knew. As did Potter's words today, while he stood there under the sheltering church-yard trees, holding Horace's folded flag.

Perhaps when Potter reads these lines, he will sense something of how Horace warmed and encouraged me. I have probably not lived up to Potter's expectations by what I have written about his brother here. There was just too much humanity in Horace for words to capture. The highest, gentlest, noblest kind of humanity.

August 27

Monday morning and I'm nervous as a cat. And excited. The rough draft is so long. I've made myself outline the remainder of the story with a loose estimate of how many pages I may need for each scene. This outline cannot hold, will have to bend. The creative process takes over unmindful of length, but deletions can be handled—along with errors—in the rewrite.

(The way I go along blithely depending on the rewrite, one would think someone else was going to do it!)

Can I finish in roughly fifty pages? If so, with luck, I will be through with the rough—Margaret's story will be down on paper—by the end of this month.

August 28

The End draws near, but The End does not have my attention today. Throughout this diary, far more often than I've mentioned. I've agitated for a title. My working title evolved into *A Place Called Hibernia*. Most on whom I tried it out, liked it, but none were lyrical. Nor was I. One day, during a telephone conversation with Eileen Humphlett, I tried out *A Place Called Hibernia*. She didn't dislike it, but said plainly that it did not turn her on. Eileen has typed this diary and will type the novel eventually if Elsie isn't up to it, but she hasn't seen it yet and has no idea of the story line. That is exactly the point. A reader wanders into a bookstore, picks up a book, in part at least, because of the title. The reader at the time of purchase knows nothing of the contents. Titles are important. Maria was just right for my novel *Maria*. *Don Juan McQueen* was right. But *Margaret*? *Margaret* is just not strong enough to fly alone as a title. And yet, the novel is predominantly Margaret's story. In fact, Ei- leen tells me that's what I've called it all through this diary—in twenty-one places, to be exact—*Margaret's story*.

This afternoon, in conversation once more with Eileen, she asked why I didn't just call it Margaret's Story? She must have thought I had vanished from the earth. I was stunned. Silent. Why not? The word story in a title is a natural. Margaret's Story tells that potential reader not only that the novel contains the story of a woman named Margaret, but that hers must be an absorbing story or no author would spend all that time and energy on it. For an hour, I made more calls—growing more elated by the minute that Eileen was so smart when I had been so dense. I called local booksellers to ask their opinion, then Faith Brunson, Rich's knowledgeable book buyer in Atlanta. All agreed, when I gave them the choice of the two titles, that it *had* to be *Margaret's Story*. I then called my editor. Peg Cameron. Peg made it unanimous. Dena also agreed with enthusiasm, as did Hester. And so, nearing The End of the rough draft, I have a title at last. *Margaret's Story*.

Titles are weird. Finding one is often nerve-wracking. Trying this and that combination of words, wondering how corny one can get, and so on. For my novel *Lighthouse*, there seemed to be no other. *The Beloved Invader* " came to me" while I waited in a doctor's office. *New Moon Rising*—the last line in the novel—was "discovered" by someone in a sales meeting at Lippincott, long after the novel was finished.

Why is *Margaret's Story* a good title when Margaret is not?

I don't know.

Faith Brunson said: "*A Place Called Hibernia* sounds as though anyone might have written it. *Margaret's Story* sovmds as though Eugenia Price wrote it."

Why? I don't know that either.

August 30

Today, roughly ten months from the day I wrote page 1 of *Margaret's Story*—I could finish the *rough*, rough draft. This novel is my twenty-seventh book, I think. Reaching The End of the rough is still an agonizing excitement. Margaret's dearest friend, Louisa Fatio, died "yesterday." I was so bereft, I had to call Dena.

I'll make no sense if I go on here. The End is too near.

Later—5 P .M .

I finished it, but I'm too numb to think of anything to say beyond what Virginia Woolf once wrote: Writing a novel "calls upon every nerve to hold itself taut." She was right. I've tried, but

I doubt that I've truly "let down" once since last September.

August 31
For the first hour after I finished yesterday, I just sat. Then Joyce and I began to plan ways to celebrate. True, there are months of hard work up ahead. *That rewrite won't do itself.* But the most difficult and complex story I've tried thus far is down on paper. Period. Cleaning up, polishing, (in this case) wholesale deleting, is a totally different experience. No trauma except the deadline. I will enjoy, and at times will struggle, but not enough of interest to a reader will happen to continue this diary.

"What do you most want to do as a first act of celebration?" Joyce asked. "I want to call Margaret's granddaughter, Dorothy Austin, at her summer home, in New England." I did and her spontaneity swung wide the celebration gates for me. Next, I called Dena, then Hester Williams, then Joyce's mother—and mine. It was obvious that Mother felt rotten, but as always, she tried valiantly to cheer me. When I talked to Nancy, she too, tried to reassure me that by today Mother would probably feel much better.

Of course, that put a damper on my high spirits, but Joyce took me to dinner at Alfonza's. As always, Alfonza and our other friends there entered into the celebration. Sometimes I think our neighbors in the bookstores, at Chaney's Standard Station, at the cleaners, the drug-store—are my best encouragers. And when a finished manuscript finally goes to the post office, there is a ceremony there, too. I really don't function alone except for the actual hours spent at the typewriter. I am blessed.

September 3
During the past few days of long neglected errands–haircut, pick up glasses, sign books in local shops, clean my office and straighten the mass of Margaret Fleming research material—I have called Nancy often to check on Mother. My own plans may need to be radically changed. I have made reservations at my St. Augustine motel for an indefinite stay in which I will read and mark the entire 803-page rough draft preparatory to starting the

rewrite. For weeks, I have lived for this particular time alone with my manuscript in the picturesque old city. Now, I don't know which way to turn.

A call just now from Nancy: Mother has been rushed to the hospital. *And* Hurricane David is building and heading our way. A hurricane watch is in effect from Miami to Jacksonville and that is only seventy miles down the coast from St. Simons.

Of course, David is expected to hit St. Augustine. It is noon and I still have not cancelled my motel reservations! I want *so much* to go. I need to go, but one also needs to be flexible—especially when two hurricanes are in the offing—David and Frederic. Three for me. Mother's illness strikes with hurricane force, since I must stay near an airport far enough from David's winds and flooding so that I can take a plane at a moment's notice if Nancy says the word.

What to do? A weather warning minutes ago informed us that all barrier islands are to be evacuated. That settles the St. Augustine trip. For now, at least. I've just called to cancel. Stephie and Horst are preparing for David, too. Concerned that hurricane reports might be adding to Mother's anxieties, I called Nancy again. "She is too sick to know anything about the hurricane. So don't worry at all about that. She doesn't even know it's her birthday today," Nance said, attending to me as lovingly and sensi- tively as she attends Mother. "And I don't think there is any point in your coming now. She has pneumonia, but today her temperature is down. Just stay in touch. And stay with that novel." I hung up the telephone in time for it to ring again. It was our friend Jean Alexander, from the Chamber of Commerce. The police had just asked her to urge Joyce and me to leave the Island at once. "They're up there in the woods almost surrounded by tidal marsh and with only one access road," the officer said.

As I write these lines, Joyce is outside putting away loose flower pots, swinging bird feeders and potted plants. We are leaving. The wind is wild already and the low Island sky has poured rain off and on all morning. I must stop this and run down to help haul in the wicker porch furniture before the sky falls again.

Where is Margaret Fleming in all this? Smack at the front of my thoughts! My blessed escape from anything.

September 6
Back on the Island

For two days we stayed at a favorite motel in the Georgia foothills, keeping close watch on our Island via television. The causeway to the mainland (our only way off the Island) was closed for only a few hours. We worried, as it turned out, quite unnecessarily, about Sarah Edmond, Ruby Wilson—alone in her house—and Elsie, still weak from the surgery and also alone. None would agree to leave and they were lucky. Hurricane David quixotically moved out to sea fifty miles off our coast. There was almost no damage. Power was off, we discovered by our slow clocks, for about six hours. Limbs and moss blew down, marsh reeds covered the causeway, left behind by the receding tides. Nothing more. *And*, I had sense enough to take along the 114 unanswered letters and my cassette tape recorder. By writing some myself in longhand and dictating long tapes for Eileen, I managed to handle every letter. No work time was lost.

En route home, we listened to radio from Savannah, where there was not only widespread damage, but an unbelievably long power blackout. I hope dear Susan Hartridge is all right. I won't call since hearing the plea that even local Savannah calls be kept at a minimum. I did call the St. Augustine motel the minute I had learned from Nancy that Mother is improving. David missed them, too. Now I feel free about leaving—with an extra piece of luggage needed to transport the enormous stack of manuscript.

I just stopped writing here and sighed heavily. A sigh of relief. With Mother on the mend and Nance "in charge," with David past (now dumping tons of water on the northeast coast), I can once again give Margaret Fleming my full attention. The flurry is over. I am back with my people beside the St. Johns.

And at The End of this diary.

Just where I began—upbeat and excited, leaving within the hour for St. Augustine. Once a novel is completely finished, I miss my people to the point of distraction. That is no cause for concern now—not until February of next year when the rewrite and all its last-minute refinements will have to be finished and ready for the publisher. The really painful missing will not even start then, since, after a few weeks, the big manuscript will twice more be returned to me so that I can work through my editor's suggestions, then still later on, check copyediting. Additional time will pass and one day it will be all in print, and I will have my last lengthy visit with Margaret at Hibernia as I read it once more, checking galleys.

Then the loneliness *will* close in.

But that is not today. As I have already written in these pages—today is what I have. And in it, St. Augustine, solitude and the finished rough to read. Up ahead and into the spring I will still have the rewrite, in which patches of bad writing, errors, confused dates can be smoothed out and by grace, gumption and hard work—be made to read like a novel.

Sometime in the fall of 1980, if all goes well, I will sit at tables in bookstores behind stacks of books bearing the title *Margaret's Story*. And all that I have set down in these pages of struggle and anxiety and fear and weariness will be forgotten. Almost as though none of it ever happened.

Margaret Seton Fleming, I can never forget. Nor Hibernia, her almost mystical place by the river.

Acknowledgments

Since this book is a highly subjective diary concerning some of what does and does not go on in a novelist's mind and personal life during the research and writing of a long novel, acknowledgments do not take the usual form. Not that I haven't had help with it—everyone who touched my life for better or for worse from September 13, 1978 to September 6, 1979—gave to this diary.

Perhaps I am indebted first of all to the hundreds of readers who, through the years, have asked how I go about the research and writing of a fictionized book about real people who Lived at a specified time in history. Those readers gave me the idea. Of course, each novel poses different problems. This is an almost daily account of the making of *Margaret's Story*.

Particular credit is due my publisher, Edward L. Bur- lingame, whose imaginative decision it was to publish the novel and its diary simultaneously.

Experiencing the solid, completely enjoyable author-editor

relationship with Peg Cameron through both books has been even more rewarding than I expected—and my expectations were high. I am grateful to Nancy Gilbert, who kept me in line on the mechanics—spelling, punctuation and dates.

Again, at the conclusion of another manuscript, I salute my best friend and fellow author, Joyce Blackburn. As you will know from reading this diary, I have been bothered throughout the writing of the two books by what doctors call labyrinthitis—middle ear imbalance. I know it gave me imbalance as a person. No one could be more aware of this than Joyce. She has not only weathered it nobly, she helped me weather it. As with every manuscript I've done for the past twenty years, my final version once again benefited from her superb suggestions. Before my publisher sees a new book, Joyce has already done much to "make me sound better." On the diary, she was an authority. After all, she lived through the entire year in the same house with the often dizzy and usually vague author.

My mother, Anna S. Price, Nancy Goshorn, who lives with her, and Nancy's aunt, Mary Jane Goshorn, deserve bright kudos. They have again given me encouragement, understanding and faith in myself.

Elsie Goodwillie, whose serious surgery caused part of the anxiety in the later portions of this book, is not well enough to type it, so my heart-deep thanks go to Eileen Humphlett. Eileen is not only skilled, she is fun to work with—and she "gave" me the novel's title.

I have dedicated this book to the descendants of Margaret Seton Fleming—especially Dorothy Fleming Austin, Hester Fleming Williams and the author of the privately published *Hibernia, The Unreturning Tide*, the late Margaret Seton Fleming Biddle, who died as this book went to press. To those names, I must add here Jane Rowley, Betty and John Ingle, Jackie Bearden, Nelldeane Price, Pat Wickman, Dena Snodgrass, Reba Spann, Anna Mow, Kathleen McKee, Kaethe Crawford, Theo Hotch, Edith Cowles and Jimmie Harnsberger—friends whose interest in the progress of both the diary and the novel has not flagged once.

Diary of a Novel is not a work of art, nor was it intended to be. It is simply a work about work. I confess to a secret hope that those of you who imagined that books flow upon command from an author's fountain of "inspiration" will accept the realities of my craft. And may that only add to your enjoyment when you read a book—any book—particularly *Margaret's Story.*

EUGENIA PRICE
St. Simons Island, Georgia

CPSIA information can be obtained
at www.ICGtesting.com
Printed in the USA
JSHW020756240721
17219JS00001B/37